CULTURED

MAKE HEALTHY FE[RMENTS]

70+ RECIPES CONTRIBUTED BY **THE WORLD'S LEADING** NATURAL HEALTH EXPERTS

EDITED BY KEVIN GIANNI

Copyright © 2011
All Rights Reserved.

First Edition

Assistant Editors: Jason Jeffers (www.thirdhorizonmedia.com) and Lisa Miller (www.LisaMillerWellness.com)

Renegade Health
2490 5th Street
Berkeley, CA 94710

This book, or parts thereof, may not be reproduced in any form without permission. The scanning, uploading, and distribution of this book via the Internet or via any other means without the permission of the publisher is illegal and punishable by law. Please purchase only authorized electronic editions, and do not participate in or encourage electronic piracy of copyrighted materials. Your support of the authors' rights is appreciated.

Gianni, Kevin M.
Cultured: 70+ of the world's best fermented food recipes / edited by Kevin Gianni. -- 1st ed.
p. cm.
Includes index.
LCCN: 2011916531
ISBN-13: 978-0-9788123-9-3

PRINTED IN THE USA
www.RenegadeHealth.com/cultured

Medical Warning and Disclaimer

The information in this book is not intended as medical advice or to replace a one-on-one relationship with a qualified health care professional. It is intended as a sharing of knowledge and information from the research and experience of Kevin Gianni and the contributing authors. We encourage you to make your own health care decisions based on your research and in partnership with a qualified health care professional.

You may not be familiar with many of the ingredients listed herein. To help, we've included some basic information for many of the more unusual items. However, please note that some of the ingredients are considered medicinal in nature. So, before consuming large quantities of anything you're not familiar with (or, if you have any special medical condition or are taking any prescription medication), please do a bit of research and/or talk to a medical professional when in doubt.

Table of Contents

Introduction

Welcome to the World of Fermented Foods   i

PART I: ALL ABOUT FERMENTED FOODS

The History of Fermented Foods   3

The Health Benefits of Fermented Foods 11

Getting Ready for Your 1st Ferment - Tips, Tricks & Troubleshooting . . 21

PART II: FERMENTED FOODS RECIPES

Cultured Vegetables & Sauerkraut 31

Kimchi 57

Pickles 63

Kefir 69

Yogurt 77

Cheese & Sour Cream (Vegan and Non-vegan) 83

Miso & Tempeh 93

Beverages 99

Gluten-Free Breads 117

Snacks 121

PART III: BIOS & INDEXES

Our Awesome Contributors 131

Index

by Subject 150

by Recipe Name 159

by Contributor Name 162

Introduction

A FERMENTED FOODS Q & A WITH KEVIN GIANNI

What's the Big Deal About Fermented Foods Anyway?

Since you're reading this book, you've probably heard some amazing stuff about fermented foods.

Every year, it seems as if there's some new health food craze that's hyped up in lifestyle magazines, shows up all over the web and is a hit at your local health food store. After a few months however, the buzz dies down and it gradually fades away, a questionable quick-fix that never quite did what it was supposed to, leaving you on a desperate hunt for answers all over again. Sound familiar?

Thankfully, I'm thrilled to inform you that this is most certainly not the case with fermented foods. Far from being a wishy-washy, not-quite-holistic food fad, the preparation of fermented foods is one of the oldest culinary traditions in existence, bringing with it a wealth of history, numerous health benefits and all kinds of ways to incorporate them into your diet.

Perhaps best of all, they're easy to prepare and cost *next to nothing*.

On my website, RenegadeHealth.com, we present information on how you can take your health into your own hands and radically transform your life in the process. Rather than present worn out, recycled remedies to your health problems that only mask your symptoms temporarily, we seek the root cause of so many of the health issues that plague people today. The goal? Helping you to understand just how your body works so you don't have to struggle with unresolved sickness; instead, you can eliminate what's causing it in the first place.

We've made it our mission to share what we've personally learned about exercise, raw foods, stress relief, and everything we've explored to completely overhaul our lives. It's not just about feeling better; it's about feeling as absolutely awesome as you possibly can! We take the studies and science of modern medicine into account, but at the end of the day, we use personal experience as our barometer. If we're sharing something with you, it's because it worked wonders for us.

In fact, that's exactly why this book exists.

We've shared our experiences with fermented foods on the website before, and I've been consistently amazed at how much it captivated people and left them wanting to know more; with each new post, we've been thoroughly *bombarded* by more and more questions! It's clear that many people are eager to start fermenting foods at home and reaping all of the possible benefits they have to offer.

Although it's not possible to pin down exactly why so many people are suddenly clamoring to know more about fermented foods, I think this explosion of interest sprung from the resurgent popularity of kombucha tea, a tangy, fizzy tonic that has been consistently taking up more refrigerated shelf space in supermarkets and health food stores in recent years. Like most other fermented foods, kombucha works wonders on your digestive system, and many people who regularly drink it report that it has positively affected their struggles with conditions as varied as acne, constipation and acid reflux, among others.

As I mentioned, these kinds of effects aren't just limited to kombucha, however, and there's been a gradual, spreading awareness that these incredible benefits are largely attributable to the fermentation process; because of this, so many people have started looking into what fermented foods can do for them. Over the course of this book, as we delve deeper into the history and science of fermentation, you'll see that this kind of enthusiasm for all kinds of fermented foods has been common throughout history, in every corner of the world. It's a welcome and exciting assurance as you embark on the grand adventure that is fermentation.

So, How Exactly Does Fermentation Work?

You may not realize it, but many of the foods you eat and drink are actually fermented:

• Yogurt and cheese are the products of fermented milk.
• Beer and many breads (such as sourdough) are made from fermented grains.
• Wine is the delicious result of fermented grapes.
• Miso and tempeh are made from fermented soy beans.

Beyond those you're familiar with, there are literally hundreds of delicious fermented foods and drinks you've probably never heard of.

In simple terms, we refer to foods as fermented when they have been aged with bacteria and/ or yeast. In ancient cultures across this globe, this was one of the foremost ways to preserve foods beyond their usual lifespan so they could be consumed for months, even years on end.

In the process of preparing and eating these foods, it was discovered that this method not only preserved the nutritional content of the food, but also unlocked all kinds of new flavors and textures to delight the palate. Better yet, many of them were now enhanced with amazing health benefits. With this knowledge, people across so many of the world's great cultures worked to experiment with and perfect their methods of fermentation, documenting their processes and effects along the way.

The magic of fermentation lies in how the process breaks down the food being fermented. With time, fermentation creates and releases an array of nutrients, amino acids, vitamins and more. The key to this is bacteria.

Wait… what?

Who's Afraid of a Little Bacteria?

Unfortunately, the answer to that question is: *almost everybody*! Bacteria has gotten quite a bad rap in our modern world as a scourge to be eliminated through the use of antibacterial soaps, sanitizers and all kinds of clinical means. Of course, this is sometimes necessary due to the havoc caused by bad bacteria such as E. coli and salmonella, which have become notorious to the public through dozens of outbreaks in everything from spinach to peanut butter.

What most people don't realize is that there are also healthy, helpful strains of bacteria, which we rely on to survive. In fact, we're filled with them, with the amount of bacteria in your body outnumbering your cells by 10 to 1. We're more bacteria than anything else! [1]

Your digestive system is home to billions of strains of friendly bacteria called microflora. Their job is to break down the foods you eat into a form that can be absorbed by your body. That's the process we know as digestion. As such, if you're not filled with these bacteria, you're not getting all of the nutrients, vitamins and minerals you need from your food, and that's the start of a whole host of health issues - food allergies, skin problems, you name it. There's even evidence emerging that compromised gut health may play a role in degenerative diseases such as autism and Alzheimer's disease.

Unbelievably, many of us deal with this predicament every day with nary a clue. For example, have you ever:

• Taken antibiotics?
• Dealt with a significant amount of stress that has left you feeling worn down?
• Had chlorinated tap water to drink?
• Eaten a diet laden with processed and fried foods without balancing it with fresh vegetables and fruits?
• Dealt with a food allergy?

Most of us would answer yes to at least two or three of these questions, and that presents a bit of a problem: all of these experiences have been proven to have a negative impact on the amount of microflora in our gut. As such, many people today are dealing with problems that begin in their digestive systems without ever realizing this.

This is the foremost benefit of eating fermented foods: repopulating your gut with the strains of bacteria that allow your digestion to function at an optimum level. Later in the book, we'll explore the many ways a good supply of gut bacteria sets the foundation for good health, but for now, know this: you need strong, plentiful microflora!

The truth is, it isn't just you; everybody needs good, friendly bacteria in their gut, and can experience quite a bit of trouble if they don't have it… even health advocates out to save the world…

In case you don't realize, I'm talking about myself.

Kevin vs. his Gut

I haven't always taken care of myself. In fact, it seems there were definitely times in my life when I was out to see just how far I could push myself. Things got ugly.

It didn't start out that bad. In high school, I was a co-captain of the football team that won the 1995 Connecticut State Football Championship. I was also on our tennis team as a member of the top doubles team in our conference. On top of all that, I also found time to dedicate myself to basketball and weightlifting.

Impressive, huh?

There was a problem brewing, however. Even though I was on top of my fitness game, I had **horrible** eating practices as I knew and cared little about nutrition. For example, my tennis teammate and I would get "pumped up" for upcoming matches by eating an energizing snack of Mountain Dew and Twinkies, followed up by a few cigarettes. It would be years later before I realized we were pumping ourselves full of crap.

Things got much worse when I went to college in New York. Although I was still lifting weights from time to time, overall, my athletic drive came to a screeching halt. In its place, I took up the most common extra-curricular activity practiced by most young adults away from home for the first time:

I partied. And I partied. And I partied.

As for sleep? Well, let's just say it was something I did when I had time.

This should have been temporary, a phase at most, but it lasted a bit longer for me. I lived through four years of college this way, and it continued into my working life until I just couldn't hold it together anymore. I was a washed up, burned out shell of a man by age 23.

After moving back home to reflect, I turned my life inside out and shook out the junk. The self-proclaimed "beer-guzzling loser" was nowhere to be found. Instead of chugging brew, flirting until four in the morning and hanging around pool tables, I discovered a plant-based diet, raw food, and new modalities in fitness and nutrition. I founded successful websites devoted to my discoveries and found myself being quoted in magazines and websites galore. I even got married!

Impressive, huh?

Well, even then there were still a few things I was dealing with. In fact, I came to realize that life can never be perfect – there's always something to deal with, but these are the challenges that help you to learn and grow. These so-called "obstacles" are absolutely necessary.

The obstacle I ran into was a tick bite, which at first didn't seem threatening at all. However, it soon became apparent that I was facing the threat of Lyme disease. Knowing how terrible the disease could be, and after consulting three natural doctors, I reluctantly decided to fight it off with a 21-day treatment of antibiotics.

After those three weeks, I was Lyme-free, but I had a new problem. My digestion was an absolute wreck. I'll spare you the ugly details, but let's just say things weren't pretty in the bathroom around that time. Beyond that, I had developed a terrible acne problem and endlessly itchy skin. It was unbearable.

v

Thankfully, this was right around the time I met Donna Gates, the creator of the Body Ecology Diet and one of the world's foremost authorities on intestinal health and the healing effects of fermented foods. To prevent my problems, I had tried eliminating sugar from my diet and took a bounty of herbal concoctions, but it was finally Donna's diet - rich in restorative fermented foods - that healed my gut and everything else in the process.

I wasn't just back to normal; I was better than ever before.

Up until then, I hadn't paid too much attention to what I heard about fermented foods, but now I was intrigued. I would soon discover countless people with stories similar to mine, and several new studies began to emerge about the link between compromised digestive health and various conditions and diseases. Like many other things before in my life, fermentation became a burning new interest of mine as it helped me just when I couldn't figure out what was going wrong. It got me back on the right track.

So now, I'm sharing what I learned with you.

Why Fermented Foods Matter

Our modern society is filled with conveniences that aim to make our lives easier and more comfortable. We've seen more progress in our lifetime than any generation on the planet before.

If that's the case, then why are people so stressed out? Worse yet, why are they getting sicker?

Whether it's autism or diabetes, heart disease or cancer, major illness is on the rise. The Centers for Disease Control and Prevention states that 7 out of 10 Americans die each year from chronic diseases – heart disease, stroke, cancer, diabetes, and arthritis – which are both among the most common **and** the most preventable of all illnesses in the country. Mental illness is rapidly increasing as well. According to the Substance Abuse and Mental Health Services administration, mental disorders will surpass physical illnesses as the leading cause of disability worldwide by the year 2020.

You would think there's been enough headway in cutting edge medicine and science to effectively combat these illnesses, but too often the only solutions available to the average person coping with sickness are pills, shots and surgeries that merely tackle their symptoms or slow the progress of their oncoming disease.

What if you didn't have to get sick in the first place?

There is definitely a place for clinical medicine in our lives, but because we've become so dependent on it as part of the framework of modern society, we've forgotten that we can make powerful choices on our own that keep us healthy and keep sickness at bay. It's not about becoming a health food junkie or a fitness freak, but simply someone who makes informed decisions about how they treat their body. Chronic illness is not something that we should consider a regular part of life.

The old adage 'you are what you eat' has never been truer than it is today, and it's precisely the reason why so many of us are suffering – we're filling ourselves with so much crap! It's time to turn back the tide.

Fermented foods are important because they're a powerful way for you to take a proactive approach to your health. As you'll see over the course of the book, so much of our health begins in our digestive system. In fact, between 70% and 80% of the cells that make up your immune system reside in your gut. [2] By taking responsibility for your digestive health, you're potentially eliminating the root cause of so many problems you could face further down the road, be they skin problems such as acne or dryness; or bowel issues like gas and bloating; heart disease or conditions as seemingly vague as mental fogginess.

Repopulating your gut with friendly, healthy bacteria is one of the most powerful things you can do for yourself and your family, and to be frank, preparing fermented foods is ridiculously cheap. It's certainly less expensive than costly medication or treatments.

By following the guidelines in this book, you'll quickly become accustomed to always having fermented foods in your fridge and on your plate. In fact, I'd wager money that in no time at all, you'll be a mad scientist of sorts, concocting all sorts of fermented delights in your own home. You'll be amazed at what you can create, and how good it will make you feel.

Sounds good? Are you ready? Then let's begin.

SOURCES

[1] "Humans have Ten Times More Bacteria Than Human Cells: How Do Microbial Communities Affect Human Health?" Sciencedaily.com. June 5, 2008 http://www.sciencedaily.com/releases/2008/06/080603085914.htm

[2] "BHIVA Foundation Lecture: The Role of the Gut in HIV Pathogenesis" Clerici M. BHIVA Autumn Conference, London, October 2008.

PART I
ALL ABOUT FERMENTED FOODS

CHAPTER I
THE HISTORY OF FERMENTED FOODS

Science Finally Catches Up

In 1907, a pioneering Russian microbiologist named Elie Metchnikoff published a study that found that healthy bacteria in yogurt played a significant role in the long lives and good health of the elderly in Bulgaria. Metchnikoff was the deputy director of the renowned Pasteur Institute in Paris, and would go on to win a Nobel Prize in 1908 with its founder, the famed chemist and microbiologist Louis Pasteur. With that kind of acclaim, you would think that his study would have made a significant impact in the worlds of medicine and nutrition.

Instead, it just kind of sat there, receiving far less attention than the seemingly groundbreaking discovery of antibiotics – substances that limit or stop the growth of bacteria – would garner almost 40 years later.

This didn't seem to bother Metchnikoff much. He continued with his studies, delving further into his idea that "friendly" bacteria in our intestines as well as lactic acid bacteria produced during fermentation could inhibit the growth of dangerous bacteria and illness. He drank sour milk for the rest of his life, bolstered by this belief, and essentially introduced us to what we know today as probiotics, the healthy, beneficial bacteria that are present in fermented foods and healthy, functioning digestive systems. The term, when translated from its Latin origins becomes the phrase "for life."

Here's the thing: although we owe Metchnikoff a tremendous debt for his enterprising studies, his findings were merely a confirmation of what many cultures throughout the world have known for centuries: that preserving foods through fermentation gives rise to restorative and health-enhancing properties that weren't present in the food before. Much like the venerable, healthy old Bulgarians whom Metchnikoff was so fascinated with, people from Africa to the Polynesian islands possessed this same understanding for centuries, passing down a tradition of fermented local dishes that were considered essential to good health and a good life. They may not have had scientific studies to support this understanding, but generations upon generations of reliable experience told them all they needed to know.

Lost Origins

It's hard to say just when or where the process and benefits of fermentation were first discovered, but some theories point as far back as the Neolithic age, about 7000 years ago. This thinking holds that Neolithic people discovered fermented milk shortly after learning how to milk animals by observing how it curdled a few hours after milking. Over time, they would come to add different vegetables juices and other ingredients to the milk, or store it using leather pouches made from calf stomachs. By experimenting with these methods, they were able to preserve the milk in new and varied forms and delight in the bold, rich flavors that came with their discoveries.

Another theory puts forth the idea that human understanding of fermentation began thousands and thousands of years earlier with the brewing of mead in the Paleolithic age, almost *12,000*

THE HISTORY OF FERMENTED FOODS

years ago! Mead is a wine made from the fermentation of honey, and cave paintings from Spain to South Africa have been unearthed which depict people gathering honey, further lending weight to this claim.

Regardless of how exactly humans discovered fermentation, this much is undeniable: it simply is one of the oldest practical food sciences in existence. In his book, *Permaculture Book of Ferment and Human Nutrition*, founder of the Permaculture movement Bill Mollison posits the theory that the evolution of humanity is inextricably linked to the evolution of microbacteria, and that we would not have been able to survive this many millennia without them – a perfectly symbiotic relationship in the truest sense.

Diving even deeper into this line of thinking, author Stephen Harrod Buhner writes in his book, *Sacred and Herbal Healing Beers*, that although knowledge of fermentation emerged independently in different cultures at different times, each culture attributed this new science to divine, otherworldly sources. For these cultures, the work of bacteria was nothing less than holy.

It's a theory that may seem out of alignment with our modern perspective, but when you consider that cutting-edge science is still poking around in bacterial history to determine the exact origins of life on this planet, the concept of bacteria as an almost omnipresent substance that we owe our existence to does not sound that far-fetched, even if you strip away the religious and spiritual overtones.

However you choose to look at it, it's hard not to marvel at just how powerful a role fermentation has played in human history. And this was just the beginning.

From Healing Foods to Forgotten Foods to...

With the march of time, fermented foods became ubiquitous around the planet. Gradually, different tribes, cultures and societies began to take note of the many healing properties they possessed.

2000 years ago in China, kombucha was praised for it's health benefits and regarded as the "tea of immortality." In ancient Egypt, apple cider vinegar was used as an internal and external antiseptic and is said to have been favored by no less than Cleopatra. Togwa, an indigenous fermented cereal in Tanzania, would be eaten to prevent diarrhea, an effect that would be confirmed recently by a Swedish study conducted in 1999. [1]

Later in history, there's the famous story about the legendary English explorer Captain James Cook taking sauerkraut on his expeditions around the world. In those days, scurvy nearly decimated the ranks of British sailors who took to sea, but sauerkraut would become one of Cook's favored methods to protect his crew from the dreaded disease. On every continent and in every era to come, people were fermenting foods for reasons far beyond flavor; because fermented foods could be transported for long distances, these foods encouraged the exchange of both microbial and national cultures. On a more immediate level however, fermenting food was a matter of life and death.

That is, until recently.

The 20th century and the emergence of America as the world's leading superpower have brought a marked change to the widespread use of this time-honored tradition. Although there have been fantastic advancements in medicine and technology, we now live in an age of easy and instant gratification, and because of this, the tradition of fermenting foods has become more and more arcane. In her book Nourishing Traditions, food activist and historian Sally Fallon argues that the United States has no true culture because of a lack of cultured, probiotic foods. Of course, this is far from scientific, but it says enough about the value of these foods, plus it's a frightening assertion, because American "pop culture" is slowly taking over the world!

If you take a moment to consider the great, storied history of fermented foods, you'll see that human development would be in a much different place without them. Although gourmet foods and microwaveable "treats" may make up the more popular cuisine of the day, there's no good argument for relegating fermented foods to our past; the benefits are too numerous.

Can Fermented Foods Save the World?

The term "holistic health" is a muddy one - much like alternative medicine – conjuring up ideas and sensibilities without many people being able to pin down a firm definition. In it's most basic sense, holistic health adheres to the principle that true health is a product of social and psychological elements as well as physical ones. It's a result of everything that a person has to deal with. The resurgence of interest in holistic health is largely a reaction to a society full of sick people. Fermented foods can play a part in setting this right again, even without a consideration of their many health benefits.

The food industry is an energy-intensive one, requiring mammoth factories for processing and packaging, fleets of vehicles for transportation, and supermarkets where food can be purchased. In an age where we're faced with the likelihood of energy shortages in our lifetime unless renewable energies can properly be utilized, this system is increasingly burdensome on our society. Fermenting foods at home is a small-scale operation, reducing your family's reliance on this industry. Furthermore, fermenting your own foods significantly reduces food wastage. This, along with the fact that they're ridiculously affordable to prepare and store is a seemingly small but tremendous benefit in a worsening economy that is putting a stranglehold on more families every day.

If this line of reasoning sounds like a reach, then consider this: according to a study done in 2004 by Timothy Jones at the University of Arizona, nearly 50% of edible food in the U.S.A. is wasted each year. On top of that, the study states that each year, the average American family tosses 14% of the food they buy. And if all that awful news isn't enough, the Environmental Protection Agency has reported that it costs the U.S. $1 Billion a year to dispose of all of its food wastage. Scary, scary stuff.

Thinking about these shocking statistics and reflecting upon our history, in addition to considering the small, but increasing number of people who are looking to fermented foods as a mode of self-healing (you being one of them), there's a realization that hopefully shines through: fermented foods aren't just a part of our past, they can also play an integral, positive role in our future.

A Few Different Types of Fermented Foods

One could fill an encyclopedia with the many different types of fermented foods from around the world. The African country of Sudan could probably fill a few volumes all by itself with the variety of fermented beers, porridges, breads and meats its people consume!

Instead of publishing an exhaustive list of these foods, what you'll find here is a choice roundup of fermented foods from different cultures and time periods that you might want to become familiar with. You might even know some of them already without ever having realized they were fermented. Later in the book you'll be able to dive into individual recipes; what follows here is a primer to get your taste buds excited.

Alcohol

It's OK to admit that you were especially curious about this. Perhaps the most famous byproduct of fermentation, alcohol has transformed cultures and countries throughout human history.

Wine and beer have always given rise to merrymaking and celebration, but in ancient times these potent drinks also held a ceremonial aspects as well. In ancient Egypt, wines and beers were used in rituals, funerals and medicine, and were also enjoyed after a long day of labor, much like many people do today. These drinks were said to be the creation of the god Osiris.

In fact, if you look at many ancient cultures, you'll see that there's often one particular god who is said to have taught mortals how to ferment fruits and grains into alcohol: in Greece, there was Dionysus, the god of wine, while one of the gods worshipped by the ancient Mayan people was Acan, the god of balché, a brew made by fermenting honey and the bark of the balché tree. In Sumer, a 5000-year old culture, one of the popular deities was Ninkasi, the goddess of beer.

On a trip to Peru, my wife Annmarie and I were thrilled to discover the tasty corn brew called chicha. Believed to have originated well before the emergence of the Inca Empire, chicha is traditionally made by chewing corn kernels to soften and infuse them with enzymes from saliva. It sounds disgusting, but once this mixture of corn and saliva is boiled, any germs from the saliva are destroyed. That said, we were still relieved to discover an updated technique to create this bewitching potion. It's much easier to serve at parties!

Yogurt and Kefir

Without question, yogurt is definitely the most popular fermented food today. It's been the forerunner in the onslaught of probiotic-enhanced products making their way to supermarkets, but unfortunately, many of these store-bought brands are excessively sweetened and some are pasteurized so they don't retain the strains of bacteria they were fermented with. This renders them pretty ineffective. That's not to say that there aren't any probiotic yogurts at your supermarket worth buying; the key is to look at the label and make sure that it says that live cultures are present. If you're eager to try your hand at making some yourself, there's thankfully a rich history of yogurt making in cultures around the world to draw on, in part because making yogurt is quite easy.

It's unclear when exactly yogurt originated, in part because it can be found in archaic cultures in India, Turkey, and across the Middle East. However, one thing that's common throughout these varied cultures is an acknowledgement of how yogurt can aid in digestion, calm upset stomach and ward off infection. In short, these ancient people all viewed regular yogurt consumption as a way to maintain the very best health.

Kefir is a "drinkable" cousin of yogurt made from the curds of milk that are left behind after it's fermented. Although goat's milk varieties of kefir are very popular, it's also possible to make it from coconut water.

Sauerkraut

For reasons that I'll expand upon later, sauerkraut will likely be your first ferment due to how easy it can be done. Although there are many different ways it can be prepared, there's always one main ingredient: cabbage. Although it's regarded as a dish of eastern European origin and has become a staple on the streets of New York as a hot dog condiment, sauerkraut is actually thought to have originated in China. It was here that the Tartar people are believed to have first encountered it, bringing it with them back to Europe.

There are many people who dislike the tangy, zippy taste of sauerkraut, and if you're one of these folk, don't worry: you'll discover that there are plenty of ways to adapt the flavor of this delicacy to your taste buds, whether it's sweetening it with apples as it's done in Russia or shortening the length of your fermentation time to reduce the kick.

Miso

Although many people might dismissively think of miso as nothing more than the main ingredient in the free soup that comes with their takeout sushi, the Japanese bean paste is a fantastic food with powerful health benefits.
The first amazing thing about miso is the fact that it is made from soybeans, which are notoriously difficult to digest. However, the fermentation process breaks them down considerably, resulting in delicious, healthy miso paste that can be used as a soup base, a spread or a seasoning.

Perhaps the most incredible health benefit of miso is its ability to protect the human body from the effects of radiation and the toxic load of heavy metals. This is illustrated by a famous story about a Japanese physician named Dr. Shinichoro Akizuki who treated survivors of the atomic

THE HISTORY OF FERMENTED FOODS

bomb that was dropped in Nagasaki near the close of World War II. The doctor and his staff experienced exposure to radiation, but somehow never experienced any sickness. Dr. Akizuki attributed this to their modest, daily diet that always included a bowl of miso soup. Subsequent research based on Dr. Akizuki's assertion confirmed this with the discovery that miso contains dipicolinic acid, an alkaloid that transports heavy metals out of the body. [2]

Kimchi

Kimchi can almost be regarded as a more intricate Korean cousin to sauerkraut. In a kimchi ferment, cabbage is joined by other vegetables such as radishes, carrots and onions, and seasoned with spices like garlic, chili peppers and ginger, giving it a more savory taste. It also tends to be very crunchy, and the fermenting process often calls for soaking the vegetables in brine before seasoning them again and starting the proper ferment.

It's a popular side dish that can be found in many Asian fusion restaurants, and probably in your supermarket as well. Its earthy, crunchy and peppery taste has won it a worldwide fanbase of people obsessed with kimchi, a culinary cult of which I've happily been a member.

A Few More Fermented Foods

Sampling a wide variety of fermented foods is a great way to taste the many flavors of food around the world. As mentioned earlier, every continent on the globe is home to thousands of different fermented foods. Here are a few more.

Hákarl	Icelandic fermented shark
Pulque	Mexican fermented cactus beer
Kaanga-kopuwai	Fermented corn porridge made by the Maori people of New Zealand
Sake	The popular Japanese wine is made from steamed and fermented rice
Papadam	A crispy Indian cracker made from fermented black gram legumes
Salami	Eaten around the world, the Italian sausage is made from various fermented meats and spices
Enjera	Large Ethiopian flat bread made from fermented teff, a tiny grain
Soy sauce	This ubiquitous Japanese condiment is made from fermented soy beans
Tempeh	Indonesian fermented soy cake often used as a meat substitute
Nan	Indian flat bread made from fermented wheat
Tuba	Mexican fermented coconut wine
Filmjölk	Swedish fermented buttermilk
Gorgonzola cheese	The popular Italian cheese is fermented with strains of the bacteria Penicillium glaucum
Sorghum	Sudanese fermented cereal grain
Poi	Hawaiian fermented taro paste
Dawadawa	Fermented Nigerian millet balls
Sarmas	Yugoslavian stuffed cabbage leaves
Mam tôm chua	Vietnamese fermented shrimp condiment

Sierra rice	An Ecuadorean fermented dish made from unhusked rice
Oncom	Indonesian fermented peanut cake
Fish sauce	This staple of Southeast Asian cuisine is often made from fermented anchovies
Kenkey	Ghanaian Fermented corn gruel
Meitzauza	Fermented soybean cake popular in China and Taiwan
Tofu	Chinese fermented bean curd

SOURCES

[1] "Enteropathogenic bacteria in faecal swabs of young children fed on lactic acid-fermented cereal gruels." Kingamkono, R., Sjörgren E., Svanberg U. February 1999. Department of Food Science and Nutrition, Tanzania Food and Nutrition Centre

[2] "Wild Fermentation." Katz, Sandor Ellix. Chelsea Green Publishing Company. 2003

[3] "Probiotic Foods for Good Health" Trum Hunter, Beatice. Basic Health Publications. 2008

CHAPTER II
HEALTH BENEFITS OF FERMENTED FOODS

Breaking it All Down

Now that we've seen how fermented foods have been used throughout history, it's time to get down to the nitty gritty. It's clear that despite where or when they were being eaten, there's always been some awareness of the plentiful health benefits they offer. Regardless of the techniques that were used or the foods that were preserved, fermented foods have helped people around the world maintain their health for centuries now, well before the advent of modern medicine.

But what exactly is so great about them? What are the unique traits that make fermented foods so fantastic for our health? And what exactly are probiotics anyway?

In our modern age, we now have the luxury of being able to discover, analyze and unfold the complex science of digestion, as well as just what fermented foods do to keep it working so efficiently. We touched on the importance of digestion in the introduction; now we're going to break it down bit by bit. It's a quick tour through the churning, microscopic universe inside your gut that literally keeps you going.

Digestion 101

Admit it: you don't spend too much time thinking about digestion. It might be something you've been paying attention to recently, but unless you've been living for some time with a specific digestive issue – irritable bowel syndrome, constipation, gas, bloating, acid reflux, etc. – digestion isn't something you've been giving much thought to for most of your life.

Don't worry; you haven't committed *too* heinous a crime. That said, it is worth a closer look to develop a basic understanding of how it all works.

The average person has an idea about how many other parts of the body work, but most people take digestion for granted. It's only recently that it's started being appreciated on a larger scale, and the spotlight is well deserved. The truth is that it's one of the most fundamental processes our body carries out.

You probably eat, on average, three times a day, at which point your meal makes a winding journey from your mouth, through your stomach, and down to your intestine. Once there, intestinal microflora – the tiny, friendly bacteria living in your gut - break down your meals and convert them into a form that can easily be absorbed by your body. It's how you get your vitamins, minerals, nutrients and nothing less than the basic energy you need to live.

Think of your body like brand new car. You happily drive it around every day to work, school or various errands, giving little thought to how the intricate mechanics under the hood are being powered by the gasoline, oil and even water flowing through its engine and steel core. It's virtually a seamless process, but as you put heavy mileage on the car by driving up and down the freeway each day, you have to get a tune up every now and then. Furthermore, you have to be mindful of the quality of gas and oil you fill it with. Failure to do this type of maintenance

HEALTH BENEFITS OF FERMENTED FOODS

can make all the difference between a reliable, immaculately preserved vehicle or a rusty, run down bucket of bolts.

The problem is that many of us today live at a pace that makes it difficult to maintain our bodies as we should. We eat packaged, preservative-laden, processed foods with little nutritional content, barely get enough rest, and when we inevitably become sick, we take medication such as antibiotics that often do just as much harm as good by killing off both the sickness we've come down with as well as the healthy microflora that breaks down our food. As if all this isn't enough, the presence of environmental toxins is steadily increasing in the world around us and they wear us down even more. Just coping with the sheer stress of it all becomes a silent, daily ordeal.

Meanwhile, you're still eating, but your microflora are dying off, slowly, but surely. Now your immune system is compromised, and you've become a sitting duck for a whole host of health problems, from food allergies and G.E.R.D. to all kinds of mental health issues.

Intimidating?

Yes, but the scariest part is that this is perhaps a spot-on description of the lives of most of the people you know, including yourself.

We've become accustomed to a standard of living and health that is far below what we deserve and are capable of maintaining. You're spared from life-threatening and debilitating diseases by the luck of the draw – you just get them, or you don't. All of this is "normal." It's also unnecessary.

That said, rather than taking time to catalogue all of the terrible things that will happen if you continue down this path, let's take a look at the incredible ways that fermentation can keep your engine purring. Right off the bat, there are three health properties that fermented foods possess that you should know about:

• They add beneficial bacteria to our gut and promote the growth of intestinal microflora.
• They provide and create B vitamins upon digestion.
• They reduce the amount of inflammation in the body.
• They aid in protein absorption and the delivery and creation of amino acids.

Why does this stuff matter? Let's tackle them one by one.

Fermented Foods Encourage the Growth of Friendly Microbacteria

So you've practically decimated all of those friendly bugs in your gut, and your body's feeling the strain. How do you get them back in there again?

As stated earlier, this might be the most awesome thing about fermented foods: they're teeming with healthy bacteria that not only take up residence in your gut and help you properly digest your food, they also help your body fight off dangerous, pathogenic bacteria that are the start of all kinds of infection and disease.

When food ferments, lactic microbial organisms start to spontaneously emerge from the food. In this acidic state, bacteria that would normally cause food spoilage die off, allowing your fermenting food to remain stored for extensive periods of time and remain edible. This transformation leaves only the beneficial bacteria that are so good to your gut.

It's astounding how many strains of bacteria are present in fermented foods, as well as your stomach. We're talking well over a thousand here. It's impossible to remember the names of all of them, but microbial scientists have developed a standardized classification system by which to identify these microbacteria by strains and sub-strains. Their names are derived from Latin, and while it would be ridiculous to expect anyone (that being you) to take a Latin course to familiarize yourself with these strains, there are a few that should and probably will become to familiar to you. Here's a quick lesson in microbacteria (and just a teensy bit of Latin.)

Lactobacillus

The members of Lactobacillus family are the celebrities of the probiotic world, gracing the packages of many yogurt and kefir bottles that have found their way to a supermarket near you as of late. Including such stars as *L. acidophilus* and *L. reuteri*, the Lactobacillus strains are known to protect against diarrhea, constipation and play an enhanced role in balancing intestinal microflora, among other benefits.

Streptococcus

The world of streptococcus provides us with a perfect example of both good bacteria and bad bacteria. While many people are familiar with strep throat, a painful, infectious form of sore throat that's caused by a member of the Group A subset of the Streptococcus family, other strains such as *S. thermophilus* are known to hinder the impact of carcinogens, reduce the emergence of tumors and lower the risk of bladder and colon cancer.

Bifidobacterium

Here's another family of bacteria that's becoming increasingly popular. A common strain in store-bought fermented foods, *B. bifidum* reduces the effects of rheumatoid arthritis and enhances immune response. Meanwhile, its sister sub-strains *B. breve* and *B. longum* lower blood cholesterol and diminish allergies respectively.

One could fill a set of encyclopedia with the names and beneficial effects of the microbacteria that proliferate in fermented foods. The most important thing to remember is that fermented foods offer a ready supply of these bacteria that go a long way to strengthen your immune system and keep disease at bay. We'll take a look at the diseases and conditions that can be addressed with fermented foods later in the chapter.

HEALTH BENEFITS OF FERMENTED FOODS

Fermented Foods Create B Vitamins

If you take a daily multivitamin, take a quick look at the back of the bottle. You'll notice that there isn't just one B vitamin, but several. Here's the whole gang, as well as their individual specialties:

- Thiamine (B1) aids the body in producing energy and stimulates the enzymes that affect the nerves, heart and muscles.
- Riboflavin (B2) functions much the same as Thiamine.
- Niacin (B3) also produces energy for the body and plays a major role in skin and digestive health, in addition to promoting a properly functioning nervous system.
- Pantothenic acid (B5) is necessary for growth and development.
- Pyridoxine (B6) aids maintenance of healthy red blood cells, the nervous system and sections of the immune system. It also helps to break down protein.
- Biotin (B7), like B6, helps to break down protein as well as carbohydrates and aids in the production of hormones.
- Folic acid (B9) helps the cells in the body make and maintain DNA and is essential for the production of red blood cells.
- Cobalamin (B12) regulates how the body uses folic acid and carbohydrates, and is critical for growth, the production of red blood cells, and the healthy functioning of the body's nervous system.

In short, they're *absolutely* essential for a healthy body.

You can find B vitamins in foods such as spinach, eggs and many types of peas and beans, but they're especially abundant in fermented foods, forming as the healthy microbes that are present begin to mature. As if that wasn't fantastic enough, these microbial cultures, once present in the gut, spur on the body to *naturally produce* its own stock of B vitamins.

Bet your multivitamin can't do that.

As it stands, pill form is not the best way to get any kind of vitamin. Although multivitamins aren't useless, they're inefficient, presenting vitamins as mere chemicals, typically in limited amounts. The body is used to recognizing vitamins as constituent parts of whole foods, 'prepackaged' with enzymes and nutrients that help them to get to work in your body correctly. As such, it's always preferable to make sure you're eating a diet full of healthy, whole foods that provide you with the many different types of vitamins you need.

With this being the case, what better way to do so than through fermented foods? Not only do they contain the vitamins you need, they practically turn you into a B vitamin factory!

Fermented Foods Reduce the Amount of Inflammation in the Body

Your experience with inflammation probably hasn't been a pleasant one, be it a bruised swollen toe or inflamed gums. What you probably don't realize is that this is a beneficial reaction your body uses to respond to infection or injury; it's a natural healing process that we should be thankful for.

Too much of a good thing is often bad for you, however, and this is certainly the case with inflammation. Many people live with chronic low-grade inflammation throughout their body, and increasing studies such a recent one done by Virginia Tech show that this can lead to the cause of many health conditions such as health disease, diabetes and arthritis. According to the university's research, some of the main inflammatory agents in the body are bacteria called microbial endotoxin, and they have been found in mildly elevated levels in the systems of many patients with major diseases. [6]

Fermented foods are strong weapons in the fight against inflammation due to their ability to help rebuild your immune system, thus reducing the strength of the minor infections that keep the inflammation in your body at a sustained level. Furthermore, the beneficial bacteria that find their way into your gut through fermented foods are able to displace and destroy the microscopic, harmful bacteria that your body may constantly be at war with, a fight that makes you more susceptible to diseases of all sorts.

Fermented Foods Encourage Protein Absorption and the Delivery and Creation of Amino Acids

Everybody's heard of amino acids, but few people know how they truly work. They're some of the body's secret weapons, essential building blocks in the creation of every animal that has ever walked the face of the earth – including us humans. They *really* don't get enough credit.

What does get a lot of attention is protein, in all its myriad forms. Proteins are absolutely necessary, but not in the way that most people think they are. We have the fitness industry to thank for the widespread appreciation of a protein-rich diet, but there's still a basic misunderstanding in the general public about just why proteins are so essential.

Proteins do help your body build muscle and repair itself on a daily basis, but it's an intricate process. Proteins are actually constructed from amino acids. When digested they're broken back down into amino acids, which are then whisked away to the parts of the body where they're needed… which is everywhere!

• Amino acids are responsible for the production of neurotransmitters which regulate brain function and various aspects of your mental health
• Amino acids are essential for the production and maintenance of many different types of tissues, glands, hormones and enzymes in your body
• Amino acids are responsible for the construction of blood protein, and the reconstitution of protein throughout the body.
• Amino Acids serve as a source of energy for the body.

There are 23 amino acids in all, eight of which are essential. This is a bit of a misleading term, as it's used to denote the fact that we can only get these amino acids from a food source. The remaining 15 are absolutely necessary as well, however, but will be produced by our body provided you are receiving a steady dose of essential amino acids.

So where do fermented foods come into the picture?

One of the great benefits of fermented foods is that they are "pre-digested", meaning our body doesn't have to expend any energy breaking them down to unlock the goodness contained within. For people who may have a compromised digestive system, digesting proteins can be problematic as their microflora are not diverse or strong enough to break down the proteins they eat in order to receive the amino acids they need. For these people, fermented foods are a godsend as they allow them to absorb protein, and ultimately amino acids – as well as other nutrients - very, very easily. Even if your digestion is functioning pretty well, fermented foods still provide the benefit of sparing your body the energy intensive task of extracting amino acids from your meals. They're just there and ready to go.

What Fermented Foods Are Good For

If you understand just what fermented foods do once they're inside your body, then you can deduce just how many ways they can help you. Still, it's nice to know what conditions or diseases they can help you stave off or reduce the symptoms of.

Fermented foods shouldn't be thought of as miracle cures, but rather mega-powered foods that enhance your overall health, reducing your chances of getting sick in the first place, or aiding in your recovery. They're part of a revamped life for many of us, one in which you don't wait until you're seriously ailing to address what's going wrong with you. It's all about prevention.

Heart Disease

Heart disease is the leading cause of death in America and has been for some time. Sadly, many people with cardiovascular disease go undiagnosed or/and untreated. It's practically an epidemic.

One of the main culprits in the realm of cardiovascular health is cholesterol, which the body naturally produces in the liver, but which we also receive through many animal-based foods such as dairy, meat and eggs. When there's too much cholesterol in the body, there's a serious problem brewing as it calcifies in the arteries, restricting and even blocking blood flow to the heart. If blood flow ceases to even a single region of the heart, then you have a heart attack.

According to a study done in 2010 by Rural Dental College in Maharashtra, India [1], probiotics – defined by the World Health Organization as "live microorganisms, which, when administered in adequate amounts, confer a health benefit on the host," a definition that includes fermented foods as we're discussing them – create acids that counter the production of cholesterol in the liver, and even break down existing cholesterol and use it for nourishment.

Of course, all of the standard-issue advice on maintaining heart health still applies – go easy on the animal products (or eliminate them altogether if you can), try not to overdo sugar and salt in your diet, and get regular exercise. These are guiding principles of good health in general, and when combined with fermented foods, they can help you fend off life-threatening cardiac issues.

Skin Health

Although skin health might not seem like a major health issue to some, it covers a wide range of conditions that are a source of daily torment for many people. Whether it's acne or psoriasis, or even premature wrinkles, unhealthy skin is something that far too many people have to deal with.

Because the skin is the body's largest organ, imbalanced internal health is quick to be mirrored in unhealthy looking skin, be it in the form of dermatitis, eczema or simply pale, ghostly tone. Bleh!

For example, a study published in January 2011 by Whitney P. Bowe from the State University of New York and Alan C. Logan of the Integrative Care Centre of Toronto collected and confirmed the findings of previous study done in Russia that found that 54% of patients with acne were found to have an imbalance of intestinal microbacteria. While it doesn't go as far as to say that acne is a disease of the gut, it does confirm that "gut microbes, and the integrity of the gastrointestinal tract itself, are contributing factors in the acne process."[2]

Amino acids also play a crucial role in skin health, as they're responsible for the formation of collagen, a protein that is responsible for keeping skin taut and youthful.

As we've seen, fermented foods replenish the gut with microflora essential to a balanced inner ecosystem, and some of the byproducts of this process are amino acids. I know from personal experience what impact fermented foods can have on your skin, as I used them to free myself of the horrid acne that I was stricken with after a damaging round of antibiotics.

Allergies

The standard line on allergies is that they can't be helped. You're simply born with an aversion to certain things – plants, pets, foods, you name it – and you can't do anything about them other than avoiding what triggers them or taking medication to reduce their symptoms.

What if this wasn't true at all?

A fascinating study called "Antiallergic Effects of Probiotics" published in the Journal of Nutrition in 2007 by researcher Arthur C. Ouwehand found that "allergic infants have been observed to have an aberrant intestinal microbiota." The study goes onto argue that excessive hygiene may in fact be to blame for the prevalence of allergies! [3]

Ouwehand's research found that it was possible to half the incidence of allergies in at-risk infants by administering beneficial bacteria to expectant mothers and the children when born, within the first six months of their life.

HEALTH BENEFITS OF FERMENTED FOODS

The study lends weight to what many fermentation enthusiasts know from experience to be true: that a diet that replenishes your supply of microflora allows your inner ecosystem to produce a store of antibodies that can greatly reduce your allergies or eliminate them altogether.

Colon Cancer

Again, it's important to stress that these fermented foods don't present miracle cures. However, they have been shown to reduce the risk of some terminal diseases.

In the case of colon cancer, a 2006 study published in the Journal of Nutrition noted that the bacterial strain *B. longum* (mentioned earlier) can reduce inflammation in the body as well as the risk of colon cancer.

Mental Health

Mental health is a touchy subject. Whether it's widespread discomfort with the subject of seriously disruptive disorders such as bipolar disease of Alzheimer's disease, or the silent, worrisome specter of depression, not many people like to discuss or even acknowledge the presence of mental disorders in their lives.

I explained earlier how amino acids are used throughout the body, particularly how they fuel neurotransmitters, crucial components in the regulation of mental health. Let me illustrate that further with an example: a neurotransmitter you might have heard of serotonin, which is known to produce feelings of well-being. Mental health disorders such as Alzheimer's disease and autism are all linked by a marked deficiency of serotonin in the brain. In order to produce adequate amounts of serotonin, it's necessary to have sufficient amounts of tryptophan - an essential amino acid that's found in fermented foods such as kefir - as well as vitamin B6, which is plentiful in too many fermented foods to list.

This information alone is an eye-opener, but this isn't the only way your gut can affect what's going on in your head.

McMaster University published a study in May 2011 that proves a link between gut health and brain health, finding that disrupting the normal bacterial balance of the gut with antibiotics leads to an increase of brain derived neurotrophic factor (BDNF), which has been linked to depression and anxiety.

Have you ever considered how disruptive an upset stomach can be to your overall mood? With these facts in mind, it appears this may be true in ways we're still discovering.

Probiotics Vs. Fermented Foods: What's the Best Way to Replenish Your Microflora?

You've probably have been seeing and hearing a lot about probiotics recently. In fact, your discovery

20 CULTURED: HOW TO MAKE HEALTHY FERMENTED FOODS AT HOME

of probiotic supplements and their positive impact on digestive and overall health may well be the rabbit hole which you slid down to discover this book. There's no denying that they're the latest craze in the health food business.

This being the case, you might wonder why it's necessary to ferment foods at all. Why not just take a simple pill that restores all of the beneficial bacteria you need? It's less work than preparing different types of fermented foods, however delicious they may be, right?

The answer is simple: many – if not most – probiotic pills simply aren't effective enough at replenishing your gut with the beneficial bacteria you need.

When you ferment a food, you can be assured that all of the live cultures present are filled with the microbacteria you want because of one simple fact alone: if they weren't present, the food would have spoiled, and you wouldn't be able to eat it. The smell alone would be enough to tell you that!

Probiotic pills, however, go through a manufacturing process that does severe damage to the bacterial communities present in the pills. Although there are different ways the pills are processed, to date there is no method that allows the bacteria contained within to survive in its optimum state. During processing, the biofilm of the bacteria – the community structure which houses and protects the bacteria – is destroyed, rendering them extremely delicate and far less likely to survive the trip from your mouth to your gut, or, for that matter, even the trip from the factory to the store! By the time they reach your intestine, the low pH level of your stomach acid has probably destroyed the very bacteria that you were hoping would take up residence in your gut. [5]

Of course, there are new techniques for the manufacturing of probiotics emerging every day, and some brands are certainly better than others. However, fermenting your foods at home remains the best way to ensure that you will receive the microflora you need.

With this in mind, it's now time to get right to the heart of this book: the part where you start putting all of this biological and culinary magic to work in your kitchen and your gut. From all we've seen, it's evident that fermented foods can work wonders; now it's time to make them work wonders for you.

SOURCES

[1] "Potential of probiotics in controlling cardiovascular diseases." Saini, Rajiv, Saini, Santosh & Sharma, Sugandha. Journal of Cardiovascular Disease Research. October 2010

[2] "Acne vulgaris and the gut-brain-skin axis – back to the future" Bowe, Whitney P. & Logan, Alan C. January 31, 2011

[3] "Antiallergic Effects of Probiotics." Ouwehand, Arthur C. Journal of Nutrition. March 1, 2007

[4] "The Intestinal Microbiota Affect Central Levels of Brain-Derived Neutrophic Factor and Behavior in Mice." McMaster University. May 17, 2011.

[5] "The Truth About Probiotic Supplements." Bodyecology.com. June 22, 2011.

[6] "Biologist studies possible link between chronic low-grade inflammation, major diseases." Virginia Tech http://www.vt.edu/spotlight/impact/2011-06-13-inflammation/li.html

[7] "Probiotic and Prebiotic Recipes for Health" Olgeaty Gensler, Tracy M.S., R.D. Fair Winds Press. 2008

CHAPTER 3
GETTING READY FOR YOUR FIRST FERMENT: TIPS, TRICKS & TROUBLESHOOTING

Let's get to it, shall we? By now, you should be well acquainted enough with the lore and science of fermented foods that you could give a lecture to a group of friends and colleagues on the subject. Hopefully, in your own personal way, you will. Much like how microbacteria bubble together in a fermenting jar to create all kinds of fantastic flavors and probiotic goodness for you to experience, you too should seek to spin your new knowledge into an array of conversations, collaborations and culinary experiments that can benefit everyone involved.

In the next chapter, we'll get into the recipes that I use at home, as well as the wide range of ferments we've collected that have been concocted by friends and food experts who are well versed in the wonders of fermentation. Before you leap into these delights however, I'm going to cover the basic principles of fermentation that will serve you well no matter what recipe you decide to follow. Much of your learning will happen once you start fermenting foods yourself, but there are a few general pointers and philosophies you can absorb from these pages that can give you quite a head start.

Choosing a Medium

The truth of the matter is you can ferment pretty much anything: vegetables, fruits, juices, milks and meats of all kinds. Each has its own fermentation process that is fascinating to watch unfold. For the purposes of this book, we won't be focusing on fermenting meats as it's a much riskier process, but if it's something that tickles your fancy, there is plenty of information to be found out there that can help you.

Typically, most people's first ferment uses cabbage as a medium, as it's one of the easiest and most straightforward ferments to perform. From there, challenge yourself to try a variety of mediums.

Fermenting Equipment

In choosing a fermenting container, it's best to avoid metals and plastics as the acids produced by your ferments can leech toxic chemicals from the plastics or corrode metal. It's easy to find ceramic pots specifically for fermenting, but these tend to be pretty pricey. As such, airtight glass containers are probably the best options if you're just getting started. A quarter gallon or half gallon container should do.

Understanding Prebiotics and Feeding the Bacteria

The reason cabbage is so easy to ferment is because it contains its own sugars, meaning that you don't need to add anything to get your ferment going. With many other foods, however, you have to add some kind of sugar that the bacteria can feed on in order to start the fermentation process. These sugars are called prebiotics.

You pretty much have free range in deciding what kind of sugar you'll use, be it brown sugar, coconut sugar, maple syrup or honey. If you find yourself worried about the sugar content of

GETTING READY: TIPS, TRICKS & TROUBLESHOOTING

your final product, don't be; because the microbacteria feed on the sugar, it won't be present in your final product. It's the microbacteria that want the sugar, not you.

Fruits, much like cabbage, contain plenty of sugar already and won't need an additional source. However, in the case of fermenting yogurts from milk – which contains lactose, a milk sugar - be it from a cow or a goat, I do find that adding a little sugar is necessary to get the process going. On the topic of yogurt, this brings me to another subject worth discussing.

Aren't Dairy Ferments Bad For You?

If you've read my site, Renegadehealth.com, or if you're familiar with the principles of live food, you might find it surprising that there's information here on dairy fermentation.

If you're a vegan, then dairy ferments are most definitely not for you. However, if you're simply someone who abstains from dairy due to its various adverse effects on your health, or if you're lactose intolerant, I'm happy to inform you that dairy behaves quite differently in your body once fermented.

According to the National Institute of Diabetes and Digestive and Kidney Diseases, 30 to 50 million Americans are lactose intolerant. [2] Furthermore, the noted author and expert in Functional Medicine Dr. Mark Hyman has stated that 75% of the world's population is unable to digest lactose properly. [3] With those kinds of stats, there's a good chance that you or someone in your family is lactose intolerant. Thankfully, when dairy ferments, the bacteria that emerge feast on the lactose until it's gone. This is why many people who can't handle milk are fine eating yogurt.

Dairy ferments are a big part of healthy culinary traditions across Russia, India, Turkey and the Middle East. If you're apprehensive, it's understandable, but I assure you they won't do you any harm and will in fact be good for you. Personally, I prefer to use goats milk over cow milk, and regard the ferments that emerge as superfoods of sorts. Plus, they're absolutely delicious.

Do Alcoholics Need to Worry about Fermented Foods?

Great Question! Alcohol is a by-product of the fermentation process, although this isn't the case for foods such as kefir and miso. In most fermented foods, alcohol is produced in such minute quantities that it will have no effect on your body. I would, however, be careful with kombucha. Many store-bought brands of kombucha can produce levels of alcohol up to 3%, and sometimes may not be labeled to reflect this. In fact, Whole Foods Market pulled all of the kombucha on its shelves in 2010 due to the fact that the labels didn't state how much alcohol each bottle contained. [1] Many brands have since accurately updated their labels, so make sure to inspect each bottle you might decide to buy. At the end of the day, whether or not to buy kombucha will be a personal decision.

Finding the Right Temperature

Fermentation is a delicate process, and it's very important to be mindful of maintaining the right temperature in the area where you choose to let your ferments sit.

I'll give you an example: my wife Annmarie and I tried our hand at yogurt once. We were using a yogurt maker, which we figured would be pretty straightforward as it maintains a constant temperature of 90 degrees. Everything would have been fine had we not left the yogurt maker close to a window that let a steady stream of sunlight in. What we ended up with was most definitely not yogurt.

This principle also applies if you're living in a colder climate. If this the case, you'll want to set your ferment in warmer area of the house, or else your ferment may not grow at all.

Fermentation Times

Here's a tricky subject: how long should you let your ferments sit for? There's no firm answer for this, but that's all part of the fun. Effective fermentation times vary entirely based on how much prebiotic you add and what temperature your ferments maintain. With experience however, you'll come to recognize this as an art, knowing what to look for and taste for.

Of course, personal preferences come into play here as well. Many foods will have sufficiently fermented in the course of a week, but that time can be extended or reduced. For example, in the case of coconut kefir, you might like it very bubbly, which requires a longer fermentation time; less bubbly doesn't need to sit as long. Similarly, most vegetables break down more and develop a stronger, more vinegary with time; as such, if you prefer milder flavors, you might not want to allow your ferment to sit as long.

The best thing to do aside from consulting recipes is to taste your food at regular intervals, every 3 or 4 days. This will allow you to experience and understand the relationship between time the various stages of the fermentation process, in addition to allowing you to determine what kind of taste is pleasing to your taste buds.

Fermenting at Home Vs. Store-bought Ferments

Just as we took a moment to consider why producing your own ferments was preferable to buying probiotic supplements, you should give some thought as to why fermenting at home would be preferable to buying ready-to-eat ferments from the grocery.

Right off the bat, there's an immediate advantage that shouldn't require much consideration: it's so much cheaper to do it yourself! Many things are cheaper DIY style, but this is especially the case with fermented foods, as many of them can very pricey.

For example, I remember once buying a jar of sauerkraut from a store for about $9. This was

GETTING READY: TIPS, TRICKS & TROUBLESHOOTING   25

the good stuff, sauerkraut that hadn't been heated to pasteurize and "purify" it, allowing all of the beneficial bacteria to remain intact. I was quite pleased with my purchase until I came home and realized I could literally ferment almost four times that amount of sauerkraut for the same price with very little effort.

Of course, if you're buying fermented foods from your local farmer's market, there's a good chance that those are recipes that have been fine-tuned over hundreds of batches. That's fine, and it shouldn't discourage you from trying your own ferments at home. It allows you to support your local farmers and get an idea of the standards you can hope to achieve with practice.

If you're buying from a larger chain supermarket, try to look for information on the label about their fermentation practices. You definitely don't want pasteurized ferments, as they won't provide the health benefits that you're seeking. If they don't, however, and the rest of the information on the label checks out, feel free to give it a go. One advantage is that these foods will likely have been subject to extremely strict processing guidelines, giving you the assurance that the food you're getting was prepared in a very hygienic setting.

Some Health Experts Say Fermented Foods Are Bad For You. Are They Right?

As with every other aspect of life, people will always disagree on some topics. In fact, this is especially the case with medical science. Just as there are countless health advocates who tout the beneficial effects fermented foods have on the human body, there are also those who dismiss them as anything more than interesting culinary preparations.

Modern medicine loves to dismiss anecdotal evidence, but in the case of fermented foods, it's absolutely silly, even haughty, to deny thousands of years of information speaking to the health benefits of fermented foods from cultures around the globe. Furthermore, most of this information has been confirmed by modern, scientific studies done by reputable researchers. For us, the answer is clear: fermented foods are awesome!

What's the Difference Between Fermenting and Rotting?

If the thought of eating fermented foods makes you a bit queasy, you're not alone. There are indeed some people for whom the thought of eating anything more than a week old is simply gross. This is a frame of mind worth changing, however, as fermented foods are so far from the rotting foods that might be coming to mind for you. In simple terms, fermenting is great and safe, while rotting food is awful and downright dangerous! Although there is indeed a thin line between two processes, they couldn't be more different in the results they produce. Let's break down that distinction.

Putrefaction is the process that causes food to rot, and when this occurs, harmful bacteria run amok on the food in question, breaking it down to an inedible and terribly stinky state. These bacteria rob your food of life. With fermentation, however, you're exercising some degree control of the environment in which the food is placed; when this is done correctly, beneficial bacteria are produced that inhibit the growth of harmful bacteria. This preserves and infuses the food with beneficial bacteria, allowing you to eat it well past its usual shelf life.

So if you're worried that fermented foods have spoiled or rotted in any way, rest assured – fermentation has banished the bad bacteria that can make you sick, or at the very least, get your gag reflex going.

Preventing and Recognizing a Bad Ferment

Because fermentation is such a delicate process, it can be quite easy to develop a bad ferment. It's definitely something you want to avoid, as eating a ferment in which bad bacteria are thriving can produce some nasty problems like diarrhea and stomach ache.

Thankfully, it's pretty simple to find out if something has gone wrong with your ferment; it will usually be quite apparent from the look and smell!

If your ferment has gone bad, it will probably take on the qualities of slowly rotting food and will take on many of those characteristics – brown color, mushy texture, and an extremely pungent smell. If you're brave enough to give it a taste test, you should be able to tell that the unfriendly bacteria have won the battle.

One way you can reduce the chances of a bad ferment is to make sure that the food in question is covered in brine, a liquid mixture that will usually contain salt and/or a blend of the food you're fermenting. This limits the food's exposure to air and is actually one time-tested secret to producing great ferments. We'll discuss another way to avoid bad ferments in the next section.

Wild Fermentation Vs. Cultured Fermentation

Our trip through fermentation history showed us that ancient people created a plethora of ferments with few things other than basic ingredients and bountiful imaginations. In our modern age however, we're able to draw on advances made in microbiology and food technology to enhance the quality and health properties of our ferments. This is the difference between wild ferments and cultured ferments.

Wild ferments draw on the bacteria present in the natural environment, and an example of this can be seen in the traditional method of baking of sourdough bread. This was as simple as preparing the dough, then sitting it in the windowsill where it was allowed to ferment before baking. The more modern method of preparing chicha is much the same – corn is boiled, and then sugar and maybe a fruit such as strawberry is added. This concoction is then covered up and allowed to ferment. Finally, several vegetables have been fermented throughout history with nothing more than a little salt and the bacteria present in the surrounding air.

With cultured ferments, we take a pre-established bacterial culture, usually in the form of a

GETTING READY: TIPS, TRICKS & TROUBLESHOOTING

culture starter kit, and add it to our ferment, often in the brine. The benefit of this is that we know exactly what strains of bacteria we're adding to our ferment, as well as the potency they possess. Not only does this assure us of a certain level of friendly bacteria, it also results in a much safer fermenting process, as you're less likely to develop bad bacteria in your ferment.

This isn't to say that there's anything at all wrong with a wild ferment, but I have a definite preference for cultured ferments, as I like to have a good idea what I'll be getting with my final product. Furthermore, as someone who is very busy, the fact that I'm limiting the possibility of bad bacteria overrunning my food is a welcome security.

Do Bacteria Survive the Journey Past Your Stomach Acid?

Despite how powerful stomach acid is, many bacteria do make it into the gut, which you'll definitely understand should you take a trip to Mexico or India and mistakenly drink the water. Not good!

This all largely depends on the strength of the strain of the bacteria in question, and it's the strongest ones that make it through to help repopulate your gut. As such, it's important to make sure the foods you're eating have a wide variety of live, healthy, strong bacteria, which is one of the main reasons we prefer cultured ferments.

The Most Important Thing

All of this said, the thing that matters most of all is your eagerness to experiment and observe your food transforming. Fermentation is a fun process, especially if you get your family to help out chopping and packing away your foods. If anything, the most difficult part is waiting until your food is ready to eat!

SOURCES

[1] "Alcoholic Tea: Whole Foods Pulls Kombucha Drinks." Kawamoto, Dawn. DailyFinance.com. June 18, 2010 http://www.dailyfinance.com/2010/06/18/whole-foods-pulls-kombucha-teas-citing-alcohol-content/

[2] National Institute of Diabetes and Digestive and Kidney Diseases, NIH, DHHS. Digestive Disease Statistics. August 12, 2005, http://digestive.niddk.nih.gov/statistics/statistics.htm

[3] "Dairy: 6 Reasons You Should Avoid Dairy At All Costs". Hyman, Mark Dr. drmarkhyman.com http:// http://drhyman.com/dairy-6-reasons-you-should-avoid-it-at-all-costs-2943/

PART II
FERMENTED FOODS RECIPES

FIRST TIME MAKING CULTURED VEGETABLES?

Heather Fougnier Says…

Most people are nervous about making cultured vegetables at first. We are so used to refrigeration that it can feel weird to eat what may seem like "spoiled vegetables." They are not spoiled though! Fermentation is a way of preserving foods with good bacteria. The key is to "just do it" and see what happens. It's a great way to reconnect with a food preservation technique our ancestors used.

They do smell…sometimes you can smell them while they are fermenting on your countertop. That's normal! They will smell when you open them, but they are not as smelly once they are exposed to air and on your dinner plate.

Sometimes, liquid does seep out of the jars during fermentation. I like to put them in a shallow baking dish just in case.

If your veggies look moldy at the top, they were likely exposed to some air during fermentation. It's okay to scrape the moldy part off the top and if the vegetables underneath look good, you can still eat them. You can avoid mold by making sure your veggies are entirely covered with water or you use a rolled cabbage leaf to pack them down. You may need to discard the cabbage leaf if it gets moldy. Your veggies will likely be fine underneath.

The end result should be crisp and colorful. If your veggies taste swampy or look dull and colorless, they did not ferment well. Using the a Culture starter will aid the fermentation process by making sure you have a hardy source of probiotics to ferment the vegetables. Once you are more experienced at making cultured vegetables, you might try it without a starter. I like to use a starter to ensure that I get the most medicinal cultured vegetables.

Expert cultured vegetable makers have noticed that if they make their fermented vegetables while in a bad mood, the end result tastes really bad. Play some music, make them with friends or put a smile on your face and in your heart while making them. You'd be surprised at how great food can taste with this one little tip!

No experience or talent is needed to make cultured vegetables. Follow the instructions and nature will do the rest! Experience and talent will certainly add flair to your end result, so keep practicing and your tastebuds will reap the rewards.

CULTURED VEGETABLES & SAUERKRAUTS

In this section, you'll find a varied collection of sauerkrauts and cultured veggies. Cultured vegetables can be just about any fermented vegetable, and due to the popularity of ferments in the health movement, there are many creative and delicious recipes* to share. *Non-vegan cultured vegetables & sauerkrauts are denoted in the recipe title.

If you're the creative type, we suggest you master the culturing process then play around with these recipes by changing spices and vegetables to make your own combinations.

Bok Choy Carrot Crunch

Makes 1 gallon

1 ½ lb green cabbage *(about 1 medium head of cabbage)*, shredded or coarsely chopped
2 lb bok choy, coarsely chopped
1 lb carrots, thinly sliced
2 cups water
¼ cup fresh squeezed lemon juice
2 large dates, soaked in water for 15 minutes, pitted
2 cloves garlic, core removed
2 inch fresh ginger
1 packet of Body Ecology culture starter or 1 cup sauerkraut from your last batch
2 tsp Himalayan salt or 3 oz. dried whole dulse
1 tbsp cumin seed

Pour 2 cups of water in high-speed blender with the dates, garlic and ginger. Run on high speed until liquified. Add 1 package of Body Ecology culture starter and pulse to mix. Let this mixture sit for 20 minutes while you prepare the veggies.*

Remove two to three outer leaves of one of the cabbages and set aside. Finely shred the remaining cabbage in food processor with shredding attachment or 'S blade' or chop by hand. Put 4 cups of the shredded cabbage, garlic and sea salt and dates in a high-speed blender and cover with fresh, filtered water. Run on high until liquified.

Combine the two above mixtures together with the bok choy, carrots, dulse, lemon juice, sea salt (or dulse) and cumin seed in a large bowl and pack it down with your fists or with a potato masher. After packing it down, ensure that there is ½ inch of liquid brine on top. If more brine is necessary to reach that level, blend some of the veggies from the bowl with additional water in the blender and add this to the cabbage until you see ½ inch of liquid above the cabbage after packing it down.

Spoon this mixture into a Harsch crock or a one-gallon glass jar leaving about two inches at the top. Pack the veggies down into the container with your fists.

If using the Harsch crock, place the stone weights on top to keep it submerged. It will cause the juice to rise over the veggies if enough brine was made in the first step above. If you don't see ½ inch of liquid over the veggies, make a little more brine. Place the water seal lid on the crock and fill the groove around the lid with water to complete the seal. Be sure to check the crock every few days and add water to the groove if necessary.

If using 1 gallon jars, place your "homemade" weight on top of the veggies to keep it submerged. This weight could be a flat rock or a glass jar that fits into the mouth of your 1-gallon jar. You will need to fill this small glass jar with water to get the proper weight. Make sure the veggies are submerged in ½ inch of liquid. Cover it with a clean cotton cloth or towel secured with

CULTURED VEGETABLES & SAUERKRAUTS

rubber bands. This keeps out harmful bacteria or unwanted guests from the insect world.

Allow the veggie mixture to sit in a 72-85 degree Fahrenheit area for 3-7 days. If your house is cold, you can wrap the jars in towels and place in a warm spot in the house. A good location would be near the water heater or on top of the refrigerator. If it is colder than 55 degrees it may never ferment. Start tasting it after 3 days to see if it is to your liking. When it is the way you like, store in refrigerator. It will continue to ferment very slowly. It will usually keep well for 3 months or longer when refrigerated.

* You'll only have to make the starter once because you can use one cup of sauerkraut from a previous batch as your starter for future batches. Using the starter or sauerkraut ensures a hardy strain of beneficial bacteria.

Contributed by René Oswald (reneoswald.com or rawfoodrene.com)

René Oswald is an RN and an Advanced Practitioner of Health. René completed course work at the Optimum Health Institute, where she witnessed how raw foods could restore health. René has been teaching Living Foods preparation classes and seminars since 2002. She believes that everyone should have the opportunity to experience maximum health in their lifetime, and she loves helping others achieve their health goals.

WHERE CAN I GET BODY ECOLOGY CULTURE STARTERS?

They are now popping up in health food stores around the country. Though you can always find them at our store, RenegadeHealthStore.com!

WHAT IS DULSE?

Dulse is a red and/or purple seaweed that grows in cold water. As with other seaweeds, it has a high iodine content which makes it a fantastic treatment for thyroid problems. It's also packed with potassium, zinc, manganese, iron and a ton of vitamins such as A, B1, B2, B6, C and E.

WHAT IS A HARSCH CROCK?

This is a stoneware crock made in Germany specifically for fermentation. It is fitted with a special airlock that lets gases escape without letting air enter, allowing for an easy, trouble-free ferment.

CAN I USE SOME OTHER STARTER?

Culture Starters are not mandatory. Vegetables have healthy bacteria in them already that will begin to multiply if left on the counter at 70 degrees. However, there could be other bacteria lurking as well, so using Body Ecology's starter is a great foolproof way to ensure that healthy bacteria will dominate.

Scarlet Cultured Vegetables

2 lb green cabbage
1 ½ lb red cabbage
2 medium beets, shredded
3 stalks celery, thinly sliced
2 cups water
¼ cup fresh squeezed lemon juice
2 large dates, soaked in water for 15 minutes, pitted
1 packet of Body Ecology culture starter or 1 cup sauerkraut from your last batch
3 tbsp paprika
2 tsp Himalayan salt or 3 oz. dried whole dulse
1 tbsp anise seed

Garlic Caraway Kraut

4 lb green cabbage *(about 3 medium heads of cabbage)*
2 cups water
¼ cup fresh squeezed lemon juice
2 large dates, soaked in water for 15 minutes and pitted
3 cloves of garlic, core removed
1 packet of Body Ecology culture starter or 1 cup sauerkraut from your last batch
1 tbsp caraway seed
2 tsp Himalayan sea salt or 3 oz. dried whole dulse

Dilly Dulse Kraut

4 lb green cabbage *(about 3 medium heads of cabbage)*
2 cups water
¼ cup fresh squeezed lemon juice
2 large dates, soaked in water for 15 minutes and pitted
2 cloves garlic, core removed (optional)
1 packet of Body Ecology culture starter or 1 cup sauerkraut from your last batch
3 oz. dried whole dulse, broken into 2 inch pieces
1 bunch of fresh dill or 1 Tbsp. dill seed

See Below for Instructions on All 3 Recipes, Contributed by René Oswald
(reneoswald.com or rawfoodrene.com)

Each recipe makes 1 gallon

Pour 2 cups of warm water in high-speed blender with the dates and garlic (Garlic Caraway & Dilly Dulse Kraut). Run on high speed until liquified. Add 1 package of Body Ecology culture starter and pulse to mix. Let this mixture sit for 20 minutes while you prepare the cabbage.*

CULTURED VEGETABLES & SAUERKRAUTS

Remove two to three outer leaves of one of the cabbages and set aside. Finely shred the remaining cabbages in food processor with shredding attachment or 'S blade' or chop by hand.

Scarlet Cultured Vegetables: Put 4 cups of the shredded cabbage, garlic, sea salt and dates in a high-speed blender and cover with fresh, filtered water. Run on high until liquified.
Garlic Caraway Kraut: Put 4 cups of the shredded cabbage, garlic, lemon juice and sea salt in a high-speed blender and cover with fresh, filtered water. Run on high until liquified.
Dilly Dulse Kraut: Put 4 cups of the shredded cabbage and lemon juice in a high-speed blender and cover with fresh, filtered water. Run on high until liquified.

Combine the two mixtures together with the remaining ingredients in a large bowl and pack it down with your fists or with a potato masher. After packing it down, ensure that there is ½ inch of liquid brine on top. If more brine is necessary to reach that level, blend some of the veggies from the bowl with additional water in the blender and add this to the veggies until you see ½ inch of liquid above the vegetables after packing it down.

Spoon this mixture into a Harsch crock or a one-gallon glass jar, leaving about two inches at the top. Pack the veggies down into the container with your fists.

If using the Harsch crock, place the stone weights on top to keep it submerged. It will cause the juice to rise over the veggies if enough brine was made in the first step above. If you don't see ½ inch of liquid over the veggies, make a little more brine. Place the water seal lid on the crock and fill the groove around the lid with water to complete the seal. Be sure to check the crock every few days and add water to the groove if necessary.

If using 1 gallon jars, place your "homemade" weight on top of the veggies to keep it submerged. This weight could be a flat rock or a glass jar that fits into the mouth of your 1-gallon jar. You will need to fill this small glass jar with water to get the proper weight. Make sure the veggies are submerged in ½ inch of liquid. Cover it with a clean cotton cloth or towel secured with rubber bands. This keeps out harmful bacteria or unwanted guests from the insect world.

Allow the veggie mixture to sit in a 72-85 degrees Fahrenheit area for 3-7 days. If your house is cold, you can wrap the jars in towels and place in a warm spot in the house. A good location would be near the water heater or on top of the refrigerator. If it is colder than 55 degrees, it may never ferment. Start tasting it after 3 days to see if it is to your liking. When it is the way you like, store in refrigerator. It will continue to ferment very slowly. It will usually keep well for 3 months or longer when refrigerated.

* See page 37.

CHECK OUT THIS VIDEO WITH RENÉ ON HOW TO MAKE SAUERKRAUTS FAST: RENEGADEHEALTH.COM/CULTURED/SCARLET

WHAT IS COCONUT SYRUP?

Tapped from blossoms of coconut trees, this raw sap is an increasingly popular alternative sweetener thanks to its low glycemic index. It also offers a variety of amino acids, vitamin C, as well as a wide range of B vitamins.

CAN I USE ANOTHER SWEETENER?

Of course you can! Some experts like to use stevia, lokanto or xylitol.

WHAT IS A MANDOLINE?

Used by professional chefs in kitchens the world over, the mandoline is a vegetable slicer that produces slices of varying sizes and shapes for all kinds of recipes. It's efficient, versatile and easy to use.

Pickled Red Onions

Makes 2 cups

1 red onion, thinly sliced using a mandoline
¼ cup lemon or lime juice
¼ cup coconut syrup
1 tsp Himalayan crystal salt

Combine ingredients, put in a glass jar, and allow it to sit on the kitchen counter for 8-12 hours, before refrigerating. Store in a glass jar in the refrigerator for up to 1 week.

Contributed by Cherie Soria
(rawfoodchef.com)

Cherie Soria is the founder and director of Living Light Culinary Arts Institute, and has been teaching the fine art of gourmet raw living foods to individuals, chefs, and instructors for well over 15 years and vegetarian culinary arts for more than 35 years. Cherie is also the author of several books, including the classic *Angel Foods: Healthy Recipes for Heavenly Bodies*, and the soon to be released, *Raw Food Diet Revolution: Feast, Lose Weight, Gain Energy, Feel Younger!*

CULTURED VEGETABLES & SAUERKRAUTS

37

Applekraut

Makes 1 ½ quarts

1 medium-sized cabbage, finely shredded or ground
   *(reserve several outer leaves and pieces of cabbage to
   cover the Applekraut)*
2 tart, firm apples, peeled, cored, and shredded
1 tsp freshly grated ginger root
1 tsp Himalayan crystal salt

Put the shredded cabbage in a bowl and sprinkle with salt and massage the cabbage until it becomes very juicy. Add the remaining ingredients and mix well. Firmly pack the mixture into a deep glass bowl or crock.

Place the reserved leaves over the top, allowing them to extend partially up the side of the crock; put a small saucer on top.

Fill a clean plastic bag with grains or beans to act as a weight; place it on top of a saucer and put it on top of the leaves. Allow some space around the sides to ensure a good air supply.

Cover the top with a clean dish towel.

Place the mixture in a warm, dark closet for 3-4 days. (It will ferment sooner in warmer weather.)

Store your Applekraut in a glass jar in the refrigerator. It will last two weeks or more, but it is best eaten soon to ensure live *lactobacillus* bacteria.

Contributed by Cherie Soria
(rawfoodchef.com)

HELPFUL TIPS:

This kraut is sensational! The apple and ginger create a wonderful combination of sweetness and tang. For variety, add spices such as anise seed, curry powder, caraway, or cardamom.

These krauts are easy to make and very health promoting. Use your imagination and see how many great flavors you can create!

WHY ARE CULTURED VEGETABLES SO GOOD FOR US?

Donna Gates Says...

Cultured veggies are the ultimate enzyme-rich food. They are already predigested before you even eat them. They may not look like much but when you eat them you are eating food that is full of nutrients. The fermentation enhances the nutrients in the vegetables hundreds of times by making them much more available to us.

They also greatly improve the digestion of anything else you are eating in that same meal. How do they do this? As you eat them, the friendly microbiota in them travel along with the entire meal helping ensure that you digest that meal. They break down the proteins and fats, and extract the vitamins and the minerals from the food so you can retain them and build vitamin and mineral-rich blood.

If you do not like the taste of cultured veggies - yes they are sour - you can toss them in your favorite oil, like extra virgin olive oil or pumpkin seed oil. Add a touch of sea salt or other herbs and seasoning. A touch of mayonnaise is delicious too. If you are wondering what to serve them with the answer is - everything!

If you're a vegan and want some extra protein, mix your cultured vegetables into a fermented soybean dish from Japan called "natto" and you have a raw, vegan, nutrient-dense, fast food meal. You'll be eating a pre-digested protein as well as vitamins (including vitamin B-12) and minerals.

If you've eaten a food with sugar in it, pop a spoonful of cultured veggies into your mouth before or after eating the sugar. The cultured vegetables provide an alkalizing antidote to that sugar since the microbiota will dine on the sugar and it is less likely to harm you.

How did we ever survive without them?

Contributed by Donna Gates (bodyecology.com)

Donna Gates' mission is to change the way the world eats. Over the past 25 years, Donna has become one of the most loved and respected authorities in the field of digestive health, diet, and nutrition, enjoying a worldwide reputation as an expert in anti-aging, weight loss, autism, autoimmune diseases, candida, and adrenal fatigue. Donna is a nutritional consultant, author, lecturer, home economist and founder of Body Ecology™, Inc., a leading nutrition company.

CULTURED VEGETABLES & SAUERKRAUTS

Simple & Fresh Cultured Veggies

3 heads of green cabbage
1 large bunch of kale, wash and chop - remove stems and save for brine
2 medium sweet onions, such as a Vidalia onion, chopped or sliced as desired
1 bunch of fresh mint, chopped
1 large or 2 small fennel bulbs

Brine:
2 large red apples, quartered and with peel on
Stems from kale, coarsely chopped
2 tsp of sea salt
1 package of Body Ecology culture starter *(adds additional L. plantarum microbiota)*
1 tsp of Body Ecology EcoBLOOM, which adds extra food for the microbiota so your
    batches are really potent *(optional)*
3 capsules of Body Ecology Ancient Earth Minerals, which adds humic minerals to enrich
    the medium the microbiota will be growing in as they reproduce and multiply *(optional)*

Shred the green cabbage and the fennel in a food processor. Chop the kale, mint and onion by hand to desired size. Mix all together in a large mixing bowl and prepare the brine. To make the brine put all the brine ingredients in your VitaMix or high-speed blender, add water and blend well. Add brine to vegetables in the large mixing bowl, stirring brine throughout the shredded and hand-cut vegetables.

Pack tightly into airtight glass jars and top with a piece of cabbage leaf. Put on lid and let sit in a pan at a stable temperature of approximately 72 degrees for one week. You can tell they are fermented - not spoiled - because they will have a beautiful bright color to them.

Contributed by Donna Gates (bodyecology.com)

WHAT IS ECO BLOOM? CAN I USE SOMETHING ELSE?

Made from 100% chicory root extract, EcoBloom is a prebiotic, which is food for the healthy bacteria in both in your fermented foods and your gut. It can be used as the "sugar" you add to the culture starter you use to ferment your foods, and although other sugars can be used, this is by far one of the healthiest options.

WHAT ARE ANCIENT EARTH MINERALS?

Ancient Earth Minerals are a line of products that provide magnesium to your body by applying them to your skin. Magnesium is an essential mineral for detoxification and aids in healthy skin, sleep and cardiovascular health, proper immune function and helps to promote general calm in your body.

Orange Cultured Vegetables

10 carrots, peeled and grated
3 daikon, peeled and grated
4 inches fresh ginger, peeled and grated with a ginger grater
2 heads fennel, peeled and grated
Water
1 package Body Ecology vegetable starter *(you can also use another probiotic starter or some of your last fermented batch)**
½ tsp something sweet such as: sucanat, rapadura or lokanto
3 cabbage or kale leaves
4 cloves garlic, peeled and grated with a garlic press *(optional)*

Purple Cultured Vegetables

1 head purple cabbage, grated
3 daikon radish, grated
1 head radicchio, grated or sliced very thin
1 cup pomegranate seeds or 1 grated Granny Smith apple
3 shallots, very thinly sliced
6 celery ribs (or half a bunch of celery), leaves and all, very thinly sliced
1 head cilantro, roughly chopped
Water
1 package Body Ecology vegetable starter *(you can also use another probiotic starter or some of your last fermented batch)**
½ tsp something sweet such as: sucanat, rapadura or lokanto
3 cabbage or kale leaves

See Below for Instructions on How to Make Both Recipes

Warm about 1/4 cup water to body temperature. Add one package of culture starter to the water. Then add 1/2 teaspoon of something sweet to the water in order to feed/activate the healthy bacteria. Let mixture sit for 20 minutes – it will be ready when the water gets cloudy.

Combine all of the prepared vegetables except for the cabbage or kale leaves in a very large mixing bowl and toss to distribute vegetables evenly. Remove about two cups of the mixed vegetables and blend with enough water in a blender to create a brine that is the consistency of juice.

Combine starter water with the vegetable brine. Pour over the prepared vegetables in the bowl and mix thoroughly. Use a wooden spoon to pound/pack vegetables very tightly into sterile glass canning jars (the kind with a rubber lip and a clamp), leaving about 2 inches of space between vegetables and top of jar. Roll up two or three kale or cabbage leaves and place on top of the vegetables filling up the two inches of space. Clamp jar shut.

CULTURED VEGETABLES & SAUERKRAUTS

Leave jars on a kitchen counter for at least 4 to 7 days (let the weather and your taste buds be your guide - the cooler the weather the longer the vegetables will need to ferment. The longer the vegetables ferment the stronger and more tangy their taste will become and the more available their nutrition). Bubbling will indicate vegetables are fermenting. Feel free to turn jars upsides down now and then to distribute brine. If jars begin to leak, don't panic, just clean up the mess and continue to ferment.

After 4 to 7 days, store fermented vegetable jars in a refrigerator. Fermented vegetables will keep for several months in the refrigerator. (After taking a portion of vegetables out of the jar to eat, be sure to clamp the jar shut when putting back in the refrigerator or the refrigerator will smell exactly like fermented vegetables!)

Eat fermented vegetables, as a side dish on it's own, or drizzled with extra-virgin olive oil. Sliced avocado, sea salt and pepper also make an especially good complement to fermented vegetables.

* Body Ecology Cultured Vegetable Starter is not mandatory. Vegetables have healthy bacteria in them already that will begin to multiply if left on the counter at 70 degrees. However, there could be other bacteria lurking as well, so using Body Ecology's starter is a great fool-proof way to ensure that healthy bacteria will dominate.

Recipes Contributed by Julie Erwin (streamlinednutrition.com)

As a holistic health counselor and founder of Streamlined Nutrition in Los Angeles, Julie Erwin thrives on transforming private and group clients from accidents-waiting-to-happen into vibrant people. Increased vegetable consumption, in particular cultured vegetables, form the foundation of her healthy food and lifestyle programs. Julie received her Holistic Health Certification at the Institute for Integrative Nutrition in NYC.

WHAT IS SUCANAT?
A healthier, unrefined form of sugar, sucanat is the natural result of dried sugar cane juice. It's known for its intense sweetness, and contains calcium, iron, potassium, chromium, as well as vitamins A and B6.

WHAT IS RAPADURA?
Much like sucanat, rapadura is an unrefined sugar that is made from dried sugar can juice. It is finer than sucanat, but also contains a plentiful amount of vitamins and minerals including potassium, magnesium and vitamin A.

WHAT IS LOKANTO?
A Japanese sweetener that is being touted as the healthiest alternative to sugar, lokanto is made from erythritol (fermented corn sugar) and extract from luo han guo, a Japanese fruit. It boasts zero calories and a glycemic index of zero.

Cultured Vegetable-Sea Vegetable Energy Soup

This energy soup has properties that enhance your digestion and nourish your thyroid and adrenals. It is truly a healing, energizing raw soup! It's also a great recipe for when you have so much cultured vegetables that you don't know what to do with them!

Purple cabbage cultured vegetables *(or whatever you have on hand)*
2 carrots
2 celery sticks
1 cucumber
2 cups parsley
¼ cup hemp seed oil
1 tbsp curry
¼ tsp garlic powder
⅛ tsp cayenne powder
¼ tsp nutmeg
1 tsp cardamom
½ tsp sea salt
¼ cup dulse

Purée all ingredients in a food processor with 'S blade', or in a deep mixing bowl with your hand blender. Add sea salt to taste.

Contributed by Heather Fougnier (nowradianthealth.com)

Heather Fougnier, a former executive turned professional health coach and writer, is certified in transforming people's lives through nutrition and energy healing techniques. It is her mission to empower people to live happier lives by creating balance in their bodies and successfully (and profitably) doing what they love.

WHAT IS KELP?

A form of sea algae that has long been enjoyed in Japan as a snack and condiment, kelp is making inroads in the United States as an ingredient in salads, soups and seasonings. With high iodine content, kelp provides excellent thyroid support and serves as a fantastic salt substitute.

WHAT ARE THE BENEFITS OF CELERY?

Celery is known for its high levels of naturally occurring sodium. This helps re-balance electrolytes and blood. Daikon is noted for its weight loss powers. Parsley supports the kidneys. Turmeric works to support the body's inflammatory response and the liver. Ginger helps soothe digestion and guides the medicinal effects of the other foods deeper into the cells.

CULTURED VEGETABLES & SAUERKRAUTS   43

Pickled Pink Cultured Vegetables

This is a slightly sweet (and sour) cultured vegetable recipe.

Preparation time: 30 minutes / Makes 3 quarts

4 sweet potatoes
1 head red cabbage
1 cup fresh dill
½ cup kelp
½ cup fresh basil
½ cup red onion
2 tbsp fresh ginger
1 tsp sea salt
3 oz. of Pro-Belly-Otic Lime Mint probiotic liquid or coconut kefir *(You can also use another fermented liquid.)*

Shred all vegetables (except dill and basil) in a food processor (usually you'd use the blade that makes julienne vegetables). Transfer to a large stainless steel mixing bowl.

Make your brine by taking about 1 cup of the shredded vegetables, sea salt and all of the dill and basil. Put the vegetables in your food processor with the 'S blade'. Add filtered water (just keep adding filtered water so they blend completely), and blend until they are the consistency of guacamole.

As your starter, add in the room temperature Pro-Belly-Otic liquid, which is full of healthy, hardy probiotics. You do not need to add probiotics to your cultured vegetables, but it's highly recommended so that you get more consistent results.

Add the brine into the shredded vegetables and mix well.

With a wide mouth funnel, add your shredded vegetable and brine mixture into quart-sized wide mouth Mason jars (Ball jars with canning lids – you can usually get these in the grocery store very inexpensively). Pack the vegetables down tightly.

Add some water to cover the vegetables (make sure they are not exposed to air). You can also put a rolled up leaf of cabbage or a collard leaf at the top, to keep the vegetables well packed or to take up additional space between the vegetables and the top (if needed).

Screw on the top tightly and set aside for 3 days to one week at room temperature (72 – 75 degrees, but you can make these in warmer climates too). You can take the top off and sample after 3 days. If you want them to have a more sour taste, let them ferment longer.

Contributed by Heather Fougnier (nowradianthealth.com)

Detox Energy Soup

Full of probiotics, healing herbs and detoxifying nutrients, this energy soup is light, easy to digest and makes a wonderful breakfast.

Preparation time: 15 minutes / Makes 4 servings

4 cups cilantro
2 summer squash, chopped
4 zucchini, chopped
2 cups dandelion greens
½ cup cultured veggies
1 avocado
2 tbsp fresh ginger *(about a 1-inch piece)*
½ cup red onion, chopped
2 cups diced carrots
2 tsp oregano
2 tsp basil
2 tsp salt
2 tsp thyme

Purée all ingredients, except carrots, in a food processor with 'S blade' or in a deep mixing bowl with a hand blender.

Sprinkle carrots on top as garnish. Add salt to taste.

Contributed by Heather Fougnier (nowradianthealth.com)

· · · · · · ·

Spicy Zucchini Spears

Makes 2 or 3 ½ pint jars

2-3 zucchini *(I use the beautiful yellow zucs, but the green are fine also.)*
1-2 garlic cloves
1 jalapeño pepper
1 tsp Himalayan sea salt
⅛ cup kefir water *(see page 72)*
¼ cup spring water *(optional)*

Cut zucchini ⅛ inch shorter then the jar size, then into spears. Stand them in the jar, pack them tight.

Cut garlic cloves and jalapeño into spears and pack them between the zucchini spears. Everything should be nice and tight (nothing should fall out if you turn jar over). *(cont...)*

CULTURED VEGETABLES & SAUERKRAUTS

Add salt, then fill ½ full with fresh water. Now, top with kefir water above zucchini. Close lid tight and sit jar(s) on counter 24-48 hours, depending on warmth. They should turn out crisp and tasty.

Contributed by Naomi Hendrix (rawfresno.com)

Naomi Hendrix studied with ImmuneNutrition in Portland, Oregon as a Certified Healing Foods Specialist in the Fall of 2010. As Living Food educator, founder, and resident chef at Revive Cafe in downtown Fresno, CA (1807 Broadway), she continues her journey of learning and teaching how to transition one's lifestyle from a SAD (Standard American Diet) to a Real Food Lifestyle.

· · · · · · ·

Lacto Fermented Salsa

1-quart jar tomatoes *(Any size, any color. I use a mixture so that it's pretty.)*
1 jalapeño
1 bunch cilantro
1 Armenian cucumber
½ onion
1-3 garlic cloves
2 tsp Himalayan sea salt
¼ cup kefir water *(see page 72)*
¼ cup water *(optional)*

In a medium to large bowl, chop tomatoes and cilantro; dice pepper, onion, cucumber, and garlic; then, toss together with salt.

Pack the mixture in a wide-mouthed quart jar, including the juices of the ingredients. Add kefir water, then top off what space is left with clean spring water.

Let sit on counter for 1-2 days, depending on the warmth. To enjoy the salsa, I chop peach or mango and avocado with ¼ cup of salsa or just eat on its own.

Contributed by Naomi Hendrix (rawfresno.com)

"Beet It" Fermented Beet Salad

This is a very cleansing food, so begin trying it in small amounts. You can also use this mix as a dip for blue corn or raw chips, a topping for any salad or wrap, or mixed with a nut or seed cheese for extra zing. You can even make dehydrated crackers by blending the mix with sprouted quinoa and/ or sesame seeds. Very yummy, raw, and possibly easier to get the kids to love.

5 lbs red beets, shredded in food processor or chopped
1 bunch of dill
4-5 lemons, juiced
2 cloves garlic
½ cup caraway seeds
¼ cup raw apple cider vinegar
Few cabbage leaves
Pure water
1 green apple
Few stalks of celery
1 culture starter from Body Ecology*

Empty your room temp starter culture into 4 oz. of warm water, stir and set it aside.

Shred your beets and add to mixing bowl. Then, finely chop half of the dill and add to mixing bowl.

Blend 1 green apple, about 4 cups water, handful of beets, celery, garlic and lemon juice and the remainder of dill in Vitamix or really good blender. Add water/culture starter mix to your blender. Pour this liquid mixture over beets and mix well.

Stuff your outrageously clean mason jars with these cultured vegetables, leaving about 1 ½ inches at top. Roll up some cabbage leaves and place atop each jar before sealing, which helps prevent explosion. Seal tightly and run under hot water and wipe clean.

I always do a blessing or intention on my veggies; you can do this now if you choose. Ferment for 5-10 days at room temp. The longer you ferment, the more sour they become.

* Body Ecology Cultured Vegetable Starter is not mandatory. Vegetables have healthy bacteria in them already that will begin to multiply if left on the counter at 70 degrees. However, there could be other bacteria lurking as well, so using Body Ecology's starter is a great fool-proof way to ensure that healthy bacteria will dominate.

Contributed by Gina LaVerde (blissedlife.com)

Gina LaVerde loves fermented food. Especially chocolate-style fermented food. Her new book *Are You Eating Your Bugs?* reveals how these ultra healing goodies helped her family recover from autism, candida and seizure disorder. You can catch her at BlissedLife.com – where she and her family share their journey.

CULTURED VEGETABLES & SAUERKRAUTS

Red or Green Sauerkraut

My sauerkraut recipes are the old fashioned kind; they don't call for the addition of pro-biotics or cultures to create the end result; however you are welcome to use such an addition if you'd like to. Test daily as the addition of cultures may speed up the process.

1 or 2 heads of red or green organic cabbage
1 or 2 apples, cut into $^1/_{16}$ size slices
Seaweed *(wakame or other)*, several large pieces

Set aside 3-4 of the large outer leaves of the cabbage. Cut the rest up into pieces and put through a juicer with blank screen, or finely grate by hand or with a food processor or electric grater/chopper. If extra juice is extracted, add it to the mixture.

In a gallon glass jar or ceramic crock (a crock pot ceramic liner is perfect), layer the following: 1 inch of grated cabbage, 8 of the apple slices, 2-3 inches of grated cabbage and some of the seaweed, then apples, cabbage, seaweed and cabbage. If you are using 2 cabbages, make another set of layers. Press down as you make the layers.

Cover the mixture with the outer leaves from the cabbage. Weight the sauerkraut mixture down with a plastic bag filled with water or a plate with a few cans on it. Cover with a clean towel and let sit for 3-7 days, until done. You can tell it's done when it has a slight 'tang' to it.

Skimming off any foam, carefully transfer sauerkraut to clean jars and store in refrigerator. Discard apple. Use seaweed in a salad.

Contributed by Nomi Shannon (rawgourmet.com)

HELPFUL TIPS:

Raw sauerkraut is fun to make, and it lasts for up to two months in the refrigerator; so, you can make a large batch. If you've checked the price for store bought raw sauerkraut, you'll see how much money you can save by making it at home. Use the cabbages soon after buying. As they age, they tend to dry out, and you need the moisture from the cabbage for it to properly and evenly ferment.

Buying organic cabbage is especially important, as cabbage is a highly treated crop; the thought of mincing it up and letting it sit in dangerous chemicals isn't very appealing or healthy. It would be better not to make sauerkraut at all than to make it out of non-organic cabbage. Fortunately, sauerkraut isn't just made out of cabbage anymore! You can use many different types of veggies for different 'krauts'. Also, while making sauerkraut, you can make pickles. Just slice a cucumber into ¼ inch slices and while layering the sauerkraut, place in one or a few layers, depending on the size of the container. Make sure there is no wax on the cucumber.

HELPFUL TIPS:

Once you get the hang of making sauerkraut, you may never use the same ingredients twice. The flavor and visual aspect of red cabbage is preferable, but sometimes one can only obtain organic green cabbage. Here is a variation to add color and flavor to green cabbage.

The Veggie Kraut recipe has no cabbage at all! Use whatever seasonal root vegetables you can get your hands on. It is difficult to make a sauerkraut combination that does not taste wonderful, so be creative!

Also, while any of these sauerkrauts are fermenting, they can be quite odoriferous. It is best to allow them to ferment outside of the main area of your home.

Mixed Kraut

1 green cabbage
3 carrots
2 medium or 4 small beets
1 or 2 slices of onion, to taste
1-3 cloves garlic *(optional)*
1-2 tsp caraway seeds *(optional add after fermentation process)*

or...

Veggie Kraut

6 large carrots, or more
4 beets, red or white, or more
Turnip, parsnip or rutabaga *(use an amount to equal half the yield from carrots)*
1 small onion
Garlic to taste
1-2 tsp caraway seeds *(optional add after fermentation process)*

Put Mixed Kraut or Veggie Kraut ingredients through a heavy duty juicer with blank or grate as above. Layer mixture in a crock with the apple and seaweed, as in the recipe for Red or Green Sauerkraut (see page 51).

Contributed by Nomi Shannon
(rawgourmet.com)

Nomi Shannon is an award winning author and world renowned raw food coach. Nomi is known for teaching people proven steps to keeping - or regaining - vibrant health. Her website rawgourmet. com offers breakthrough information, product reviews, delicious recipes, an ezine and an online course - all free of charge.

Tangy Coleslaw

3 pounds cabbage
2 carrots
4 celery ribs
1 small daikon radish
3 parsley sprigs
1 onion
4-5 tbsp ginger
4-5 tbs turmeric fresh *(or 1 tbsp dry)*
2 garlic heads
3-4 tbsp sea salt

Chop the vegetables into similar sized chunks or shreds into a bowl. Add salt and mix throughout, using your hands to massage the mixture.

Begin packing into a one-gallon crock or jar. Use your fist or a wooden tamper. Create an anaerobic environment by getting all air bubbles out as you pack it down. Push until the brine starts to rise to the top of the veggies.

Place a saucer or plate on top of the vegetables. Try to get one that fits as close to the edges as possible. Put a weight on top of that. A jar of water works well. Cover with a cloth so no bugs get inside.

During the first week, push it down daily to help keep the veggies under the brine. Sometimes it takes a day or two to get the brine to stay above the veggies. This will help prevent mold from forming.

Taste it after a week and see if you like it. You can let it ferment as long as you want, but most people prefer 2-4 weeks of fermentation time in small 1-gallon batches. When it is too young, it still has a carbonated feeling on your tongue. This will disappear after about a week.

The best temperature to ferment sauerkraut is 55-65 degrees. Put it in a pantry, root cellar, cupboard, or on your kitchen counter. If it gets below or above this temperature it will be fine, but the best flavors develop within this range. When it is ready, scrape off the top layer and enjoy the fresh healthy goodness below.

Note: If mold forms, not all is lost. This is a test of your senses. Scrape off the mold and compost it. If the sauerkraut underneath smells okay, taste it. If it tastes off, spit it out!

Contributed by Summer Bock (olykraut.com and summerbock.com)

Summer Bock is a fermentationist and owner of OlyKraut. OlyKraut hand makes each batch of fermented vegetables, using organic ingredients sourced from as close to home as possible. As a health coach and herbalist, Summer works with nutrition enthusiasts to thrive in their own health so they can coach their clients better and create practices that help change the world!

Jackie's Juniper Vege-Kraut

5 carrots shredded
2 heads of red cabbage, shredded
2 heads of green cabbage, shredded
2 zucchini, shredded
1 lb beets, peeled and shredded
1 small bunch of celery, chopped very fine
3 cloves garlic, chopped very fine
2 tbsp fresh thyme, chopped very fine
2 tbsp fresh dill, chopped very fine
2 tbsp juniper berries, ground
2 oz of flaked sea vegetables; wakame, nori, or dulse
1 Body Ecology culture starter or 3-4 probiotic capsules, opened

Remove 3-4 nice outer leaves of cabbage and set aside. Food process, grate or shred the cabbage and other vegetables. The cabbage and other vegetables need to be processed until the juice flows.

In a crock or pail, stir in all of the processed vegetables, seasonings, sea vegetables, culture starter pack or pro-biotic powder, and juniper berries. Cover with the outer leaves. Place a plate on top of the leaves and a weight on top of the plate. The weight should be enough to raise the juice over the vegetables. Cover the top with a cloth.

Leave at room temperature for 3-7 days, depending on the temperature. A warmer environment may take less time. Check in 3-4 days, it should have a tart taste. Before removing the sauerkraut, skim residue and cabbage leaves from the container. Store in jars in the refrigerator.

Contributed by Jackie Graff (sproutrawfood.org)

Jackie Graff has been teaching raw food preparation and food science for more than a decade. An RN with 40 years' experience in various areas of patient care and education, Ms. Graff is considered one of the country's top raw food chefs and nutrition consultants.

HELPFUL TIPS:

This will continue to ferment as it ages. For best probiotic count, consume in 3-4 weeks. The lactic bacteria from the probiotics consume the sugar from the vegetables, multiply and convert the sugar to lactic, which gives the vegetables a tart taste. It is important that the vegetables be below the level of juice because these lactic bacteria are anaerobic and multiply without oxygen.

After the fermentation has been completed, strain the vegetables through a nut bag or fine muslin. The vegetables can be added to salads and the juice for drinking. This is good for a juice fast, to get nutrients and beneficial bacteria.

CULTURED VEGETABLES & SAUERKRAUTS

Super Simple Sauerkraut

1 head green or purple cabbage
2 tsp salt
Fermentation vessel(s) *(Glass mason jars with screw on lids work well)*

(Optional)
Caraway or fennel seeds
Cayenne powder
Peeled clove garlic
Peeled knob ginger or ginger powder
Cracked peppercorns
Curry powder
Cinnamon
Rinsed Silky Sea Palm or hijiki sea vegetable

Peel the outer leaves of your cabbage head off and compost them. Rinse the rest of the cabbage and then chop into strips ¼-inch thick (or thinner if you like).

Place all the cabbage into a large mixing bowl and sprinkle the salt on. Use your clean hands to knead and massage the salt into the cabbage. Sprinkle in any additional spices or flavors form the list above or add your own favorite ones.

Press the cabbage firmly into your jar or jars, depending on how large they are. I usually fill two 32 oz. glass mason jars. The cabbage mixture need not reach the very top of the jar; at least 1 inch should remain between the cabbage and the rim of the jar to allow the juices from the cabbage to "bleed out" and cover the cabbage. Using a tamper from a common blender, push the cabbage down as hard and tight as it will go, ensuring that even the top strips are submerged in the cabbage juice liquid. Place the lid on, but do not screw it tight. The lid must be left loose to allow the good bacteria to get the air it needs to reproduce into magic!

Everyday, press the cabbage down with a tamper more firmly so that no air pockets can form below the fill line. The sauerkraut will be done in about four weeks, give or take, depending on the climate of your area.

Taste test for the flavor and acidity level you prefer and then you can screw the lid on and refrigerate to halt the fermentation process.

Contributed by Novalee Truesdell (youtube.com/enovalee)

Novalee Truesdell interned at Kushi Institute and studied at LLCAI in Fort Bragg, CA. Nova has also completed Doug Graham's Raw Nutritional Science course. She first got into juicing and raw foods for when she worked in the Natural Living department stocking books on cleansing and teaching people how to follow through with those programs as well as doing demos of them. Novalee teaches raw food prep and gardening at youtube.com/enovalee.

Korean Vegetable Pickle

1 cup sliced carrots
1 cup cauliflower florets
1 cup shredded napa cabbage
1 cup purple cabbage
3 green onions including tops, finely chopped
1 inch knob ginger, peeled and sliced
2 garlic cloves
2 ½ tsp salt
¼ tsp crushed red peppers *(optional)*

Sprinkle carrots, cabbages and cauliflower with salt and toss. Let stand for ½ an hour. Rinse with cold water and drain. Toss drained veggies with the rest of the ingredients.

Cover tightly and refrigerate for 2 days. On the third day, take out ginger and garlic and enjoy!

Contributed by Novalee Truesdell (youtube.com/enovalee)

· · · · · · ·

Savory Sauerkraut Breakfast Bowl

This recipe is a savory breakfast idea I came up with when I was on a low sugar/low glycemic diet and couldn't eat fruit for breakfast. It not only tastes good, but it's full of beneficial bacteria from the kefir and fermented cabbage. It also contains healthy fats from the hemp seed oil and avocado. A great way to start your day!

2 cups raw, salted, fermented cabbage sauerkraut *(any type)*
1 cup young coconut kefir or coconut yogurt *(see page 72 or 78)*
3 green onions chopped *(green part only)*
¼ of an avocado, chopped
2 tsp hemp seed oil
Pinch of cayenne pepper

Add the sauerkraut to a bowl and pour the coconut kefir on top. Mix in the hemp seed oil and cayenne pepper. Top with the chopped green onions and avocado. Another option, for some extra texture, is to sprinkle some hemp seeds on top as well. Enjoy!

Contributed by Cecilia Kinzie (rawglow.com)

Cecilia Kinzie discovered raw foods in 2001 and was able to heal from Chronic Fatigue Syndrome and Asthma by adopting a plant based high raw food diet. Her message is that true healing and transformation occurs from the inside out. She believes that the foods we eat and the thoughts and emotions we think and feel can have a huge impact on our well being.

CULTURED VEGETABLES & SAUERKRAUTS

Doubly Red Kraut

Makes 1-2 quarts, depending on your cabbage

1 3-4 lb. head of red cabbage *(you can substitute half green, if you like)*, reserving a couple of
    large outer leaves
2 medium beets, peeled and julienned or grated
½ cup sliced onion
2 tbsp unrefined sea salt
2-3 tsp caraway seeds

Cut the cabbage in half and remove the core, if you like. (I often do because it's usually tough;
but, if you prefer, you can chop it up finely and add it to the mixture.) Shred the cabbage by
hand or in the food processor with a thin slicing blade.

Put the cabbage in a large bowl with the salt. Mix the cabbage with the salt with clean hands
and a heart filled with love. Massage the cabbage and work it until it starts to release liquid. Do
this until the cabbage feels quite wet.

Mix in the beets, onion and caraway seed until incorporated.

Take the entire mixture and stuff into a crock, half gallon jar or two, or a food-grade plastic
bucket, packing it very tightly so that the liquid starts to rise. Be sure that the vegetables are
submerged under the liquid. Place the large outer leaves on top of the vegetables. Weigh down
the vegetables with a plate, a weight, or a plastic bag filled with brine*. (If using a jar and the
cabbage is approaching the top of the jar, put the jar into a bowl. The bowl will catch any
spillover liquid.)

Cover the container with a towel. Push down on the mixture every day, and check to be sure
that the vegetables are covered with liquid. After a few days, you might notice that the liquid
no longer tastes salty but tastes sour. (This happens in as few as 3 days and as many as two
weeks or more, depending upon the temperature and other variables.)

When the kraut is done to your liking, pack it into jars and keep in the refrigerator. Use it to
top sandwiches, salads or cooked dishes.

* To make the brine, combine a quart of filtered or boiled water with 1-2 tablespoons salt.

Contributed by Jill Nussinow (theveggiequeen.com)

Jill Nussinow, aka The Veggie Queen™, is an alternative Registered Dietitian who shares food
and nutrition insights from a vegetarian and vegan perspective. She advocates a high raw diet,
demonstrating how to ferment and sprout foods on a regular basis. She showcases her work on
her websitetheveggiequeen.com and at cooking classes, workshops, and lectures throughout
the United States and beyond.

WHAT KIND OF EQUIPMENT DO YOU USE?

Jessica Prentice Says...

Culturing vegetables, like cabbage, with salt produces lactic acid and lots of beneficial bacteria, creating a probiotic health food that can improve digestion and build immunity. While krauts can be made in almost any vessel, I prefer to use a specially designed German sauerkraut crock made by Harsch. It comes with fitted stones that weigh down the kraut, and the lid features a moat that acts as an airlock: letting air out as fermentation happens, but keeping molds from entering.

If you don't have one of these handy crocks, you can use a bucket, pot, large jar or almost anything that will hold the cabbage.

The Harsch crocks are designed to culture the vegetables over the course of about five weeks, but I find that this is sometimes too long for other vessels - the liquid evaporates, and the top of the kraut can form molds. This doesn't ruin the kraut underneath; just scrape off the top and then transfer the good kraut to jars and put them in the fridge.

Eaten in midwinter, my recipe for Peter Piper's Kraut *(see next page)* is a lovely reminder of the harvest season!

CULTURED VEGETABLES & SAUERKRAUTS

Peter Piper's Kraut

Makes about 1 gallon

6 pounds green cabbage
2 lb peppers *(gypsy, bell, poblano, or other)*
¼ - ½ tsp chipotle powder, if available
¼ tsp smoked paprika
½ tsp ground allspice *("jamaica pepper")*
½ tsp ground black pepper
1 tbsp minced garlic
¼ cup minced scallions
4 tbsp sea salt, or as needed
¼ - ½ tsp red pepper flakes *(optional)*

Core, quarter, and shred cabbage finely. Sprinkle the cabbage with sea salt and massage or crush with your hands to begin to bring out the liquid from the cabbage. Set aside.

Slice peppers into very thin strips, away from the seeds. Add peppers and all remaining ingredients to cabbage, and mix to toss thoroughly.

Taste and adjust salt and spice. It should be saltier than you would want to eat it, and about the right level of spice.

Pack into a 5 liter sauerkraut fermentation crock, a 1 gallon bucket, or pickle crock. Weigh down the kraut using the stones that come in the crock or a plate with something heavy placed on top.

Unless the cabbage has released LOTS of liquid, you will need to add brine. Make the brine by dissolving 2 tablespoons sea salt in a quart of filtered water. Pour enough of this brine over the kraut to cover the plate or stones by at least ½ inch of liquid. Cover with a cloth or with the fermentation crock lid.

Allow to ferment for 2-5 weeks, depending on your fermentation vessel, as well as how the kraut looks. Transfer kraut to mason jars and refrigerate.

Contributed by Jessica Prentice (threestonehearth.com)

Jessica Prentice is a professional chef, author, local foods activist, and social entrepreneur. Jessica is a co-founder of Three Stone Hearth (threestonehearth.com), a community supported kitchen in Berkeley that uses local, sustainable ingredients to prepare nutrient-dense, traditional foods on a community scale.

WHAT IS OKROSHKA?

It is a soup that uses fermented whey as the slightly acid/sour soup base. Okroshka means "chopped," and once you've created your whey, a little chopping is all you need to complete this refreshing, chilled summer soup.

The traditional version, as made in Russia and Ukraine, uses sausage (or, more recently, hot-dogs) in place of the additional hard boiled eggs or tempeh. For her patients who eat meat, Dr. Cate explains the relative health and environmental benefits of pasture-raised, local, and humanely raised animal products.

Okroshka (not vegan)

Makes 8-12 servings

1-2 quarts of whey *(see page 89)*
1 bunch fresh dill, chopped into ⅛-¼ inch bits
1 bunch fresh cilantro, chopped fine as with dill
1 bunch fresh parsley, chopped fine
5-6 radishes, chopped into ⅛-¼ inch cubes
2-3 cucumbers, chopped as with radish
4-5 bulbs green onions, chopped fine
5-6 hard boiled eggs, chopped into ⅛-¼ inch cubes
3-4 small boiled boiling potatoes, chopped into ¼ inch cubes *(optional, skip these carb bombs)*
3 additional hard boiled eggs, chopped into ⅛-¼ inch cubes, or ½ lb tempeh *(see page 89)*

Assemble, and it's ready to eat when you are.

Thanks to its acid content and probiotics, which fight off molds and nasty bacteria, this stays good in your fridge for up to 1 week - longer than herbs would stay fresh!

Contributed by Dr. Cate Shanahan (drcate.com)

Dr. Cate, M.D., studied genetics at Cornell University before Medical School. While in Hawaii she identified four culinary traditions shared by her longest-lived patients, described in *Deep Nutrition: Why Your Genes Need Traditional Food*. In 2010, she developed T.R.I.M. (Treatment to Reverse Inflammatory Metabolism), a unique weight-loss program.

KIMCHI

Kimchi is a tradition in Korea, which has been eaten for many years. Some say it dates back to 3000 years ago. This 'banchan' (side dish), as the Korean's call it, is found on every table at every meal! It is a very spicy, cultured vegetable dish; so, watch out! You will also see these spellings: gimchi, kimchee, kimchi or kim chi.

Daikon Kimchee Kraut

1 ½ lb green cabbage
1 large head of napa cabbage
3 carrots
2 large daikon radishes, thinly sliced
2 cups water
¼ cup fresh squeezed lemon juice
2 large dates, soaked in water for 15 minutes, pitted
3 cloves of garlic
2 inch fresh ginger
1 packet of Body Ecology culture starter, or 1 cup sauerkraut from your last batch
2 tsp Himalayan sea salt, or 3 oz. dried whole dulse
1 tbsp cumin seeds
⅛ tsp cayenne

Pour 2 cups of warm water in high-speed blender with the dates, garlic and ginger. Run on high speed until liquified. Add 1 package of Body Ecology culture starter and pulse to mix. Let this mixture sit for 20 minutes while you prepare the cabbage.*

Remove 2-3 outer leaves of the green cabbage and set aside. Finely shred the remaining green cabbage in food processor with shredding attachment or 'S blade' or chop by hand. Put 4 cups of the shredded cabbage in a high-speed blender and cover with fresh, filtered water. Run on high until liquified.

Combine the two above mixtures together with the napa cabbage, carrots, daikon radishes, lemon juice, sea salt (or dulse), cumin seeds and cayenne in a large bowl and pack it down with your fists or with a potato masher. After packing it down, ensure that there is ½ inch of liquid brine on top. If more brine is necessary to reach that level, blend some of the veggies from the bowl with additional water in the blender and add this to the cabbage until you see ½ inch of liquid above the cabbage after packing it down.

Spoon this mixture into a Harsch crock or a one-gallon glass jar, leaving about two inches at the top. Pack the veggies down into the container with your fists.

If using the Harsch crock, place the stone weights on top to keep it submerged. It will cause the juice to rise over the veggies if enough brine was made in the first step above. If you don't see ½ inch of liquid over the veggies, make a little more brine. Place the water seal lid on the crock, and fill the groove around the lid with water to complete the seal. Be sure to check the crock every few days and add water to the groove if necessary.

If using 1 gallon jars, place your "homemade" weight on top of the veggies to keep it submerged. This weight could be a flat rock or a glass jar that fits into the mouth of your 1-gallon jar. You will need to fill this small glass jar with water to get the proper weight. Make sure the veggies are submerged in 1/2 inch of liquid. Cover it with a clean cotton cloth or towel secured with rubber bands. This keeps out harmful bacteria or unwanted guests from the insect world. *(cont...)*

KIMCHI

Allow the veggie mixture to sit in a 72-85 degree Fahrenheit area for 3-7 days. If your house is cold, you can wrap the jars in towels and place in a warm spot in the house. A good location would be near the water heater or on top of the refrigerator. If it is colder than 55 degrees it may never ferment. Start tasting it after 3 days to see if it is to your liking. When it is the way you like, store in refrigerator. It and it will continue to ferment very slowly. It will usually keep well for 3 months or longer when refrigerated.

* You'll only have to make the starter once because you can use one cup of sauerkraut from a previous batch as your starter for future batches. Using the starter or sauerkraut ensures a hardy strain of beneficial bacteria.

Contributed by René Oswald (reneoswald.com)

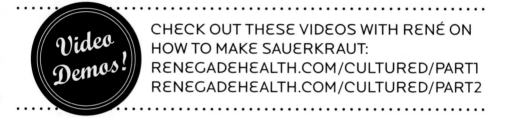

CHECK OUT THESE VIDEOS WITH RENÉ ON HOW TO MAKE SAUERKRAUT:
RENEGADEHEALTH.COM/CULTURED/PART1
RENEGADEHEALTH.COM/CULTURED/PART2

Basic Kim Chee

Makes 2 quarts

1 head napa cabbage, finely shredded
1 tbsp fresh ginger root, grated
1 small daikon radish, shredded
¼ red onion, minced
1 red chili pepper, seeded and very finely julienned *(more if you like it HOT!)*
1 tsp Himalayan crystal salt
1 tsp garlic, crushed
Dash cayenne

Put the cabbage in a glass bowl with the salt and gently massage to release the cabbage juice. Continue to massage until the cabbage is literally floating in juice.

Add the other ingredients and mix well, using clean or gloved hands.

Firmly pack the mixture with all the juice into a gallon glass jar and put a pint-sized, water filled, tightly covered glass jar on top to keep the mixture from floating to the top while it is fermenting. The mixture must remain submerged in the juice.

(cont...)

Cover with a clean tea towel and set in a warm (not hot) place for a few days to ferment. If the environment is hot, the Kim Chee could be ready in 2 days and if it is cool, your Kim Chee could take a week or more to ferment. Check it after 2 days and every day thereafter until it achieves the right tartness and spiciness for your palate. Once it has fermented sufficiently, cover it with a tight fitting lid and refrigerate for up to one month

Remember to enjoy your Kim Chee at any ripeness. The right amount of ferment is subjective – it all depends on how sour and soft you like it!

Contributed by Cherie Soria (cheriesoria.com)

· · · · · · ·

Sprout Kim Chee

I got all my tips and tricks for this recipe from a wonderful Korean lady!

Dressing:
24 garlic cloves
1 tbsp cayenne pepper
1 cup ginger juice
3 tbsp sea salt

Vegetables:
24 carrots, sliced thin
8 daikon radishes, sliced thin
2 heads cabbage, sliced thin
1 head bok choy, sliced thin
4 bunches spring onions, sliced thin

Place garlic cloves, cayenne pepper, ginger juice, and salt in blender and blend well.

Place bok choy, cabbage, carrots, and spring onions in a bowl and pour dressing over, stirring well.

To ferment this mixture, place in a ceramic or glass container and place a weight (a stack of bowls or plates will do) until the liquid rises over the vegetables. Cover this with a cloth and leave at room temperature for 3-5 days. The length of time will depend on the room temperature. The warmer the temperature, the fewer days will be required for fermentation.

Contributed by Jackie Graff (sproutrawfood.org)

Watermelon Rind Kimchi

2 lb watermelon rind
4 cloves garlic, minced
2 to 3 tbsp Korean chili powder *(see note below)*
1 tbsp unrefined sea salt
1 inch piece fresh ginger root
1 tbsp unrefined sugar
2-3 green onions, chopped, or 1 small onion, chopped *(optional)*

Cut the outer rind off the watermelon, cut into small pieces, put into a bowl and sprinkle with the salt. Let sit for an hour.

Grate the ginger into the mixture, add the garlic and onion. Sprinkle with the chili powder. Using a gloved hand or spoon, toss the mixture until it is well coated with the chili powder.

Stir in the sugar or agave and put into a jar.

Let sit, covered, at room temperature for one to three days, until fermented. Eat what you want and store the rest in the refrigerator for a week or two where it will continue to ferment.

Contributed by Jill Nussinow
(theveggiequeen.com)

HELPFUL TIPS:

Buy organic, so that you aren't eating pesticides or wax. Buy local, so that it tastes great.

If you cannot get Korean chili powder, you can use another chili powder or chili flakes, but the flavor will be much different.

If you don't have watermelon rind, you can do a similar thing with cucumbers, but you want to toss some of the liquid from the salt soak, and then proceed. The fermentation may take longer, too.

CULTURED: HOW TO MAKE HEALTHY FERMENTED FOODS AT HOME

HELPFUL TIP:

If mold forms, not all is lost. This is a test of your senses. Scrape off the mold and compost it. If the sauerkraut underneath smells okay, taste it. If it tastes off, spit it out!

WHAT ARE THE BENEFITS OF TURMERIC?

Turmeric is known for its connective tissue supporting properties. It is helpful for the liver and positively effects the inflammation response in the body. Daikon is noted for its weight loss powers. Ginger and chili flakes help guide the medicinal effects of the other foods deep into the cells of the body.

Spicy Turmeric Chee

3 pounds napa cabbage
1 daikon
3 carrots
2 onions
4 cloves garlic
4 tbsp red chili flakes
4 tbsp ginger
3-4 tbsp sea salt

Chop the vegetables into similar sized chunks or shreds into a bowl. Add salt and mix throughout, using your hands to massage the mixture.

Begin packing into a one-gallon crock or jar. Use your fist or a wooden tamper. Create an anaerobic environment by getting all air bubbles out as you pack it down.

Push until the brine starts to rise to the top of the veggies. Place a saucer or plate on top of the vegetables. Try to get one that fits as close to the edges as possible. Put a weight on top of that. A jar of water works well. Cover with a cloth so no bugs get inside.

During the first week, push it down daily to help keep the veggies under the brine. This will help prevent mold from forming.

Taste it after a week and see if you like it. You can let it ferment as long as you want, but most people prefer 2-4 weeks of fermentation time in small one-gallon batches. When it is too young, it still has a carbonated feeling on your tongue. This will disappear after about a week.

The best temperature to ferment sauerkraut is 55-65 degrees. If it gets below or above this temperature it will be fine, but the best flavors develop within this range. When it is ready, scrape off the top layer and enjoy the fresh healthy goodness below.

Contributed by Summer Bock
(OlyKraut.com)

PICKLES

If you didn't know, all the recipes so far have been "pickled." The definition of pickling is: a solution of brine or vinegar, often spiced, for preserving and flavoring food. So cucumbers, while they're the star of this chapter, aren't the only things you can pickle*.

*Non-vegan pickles are denoted in the recipe title.

Fermented Dill Pickles

½ cup salt *(Himilayan, Celtic or sea salt)*
1 gallon distilled water
3 lb pickling cucumbers, washed with filtered water
¼ cup pickling spices
3 cloves garlic, crushed
1 large bunch dill weed, washed
1 tsp dill seed
3 probiotic capsules *(with 8-10 or more different lactic bacteria)*

Combine the salt and water in a pitcher and stir until the salt is dissolved.

Place the pickling spices, dill seed, garlic and dill weed into a gallon crock, glass jar or food grade plastic container and add the cucumbers.

Pour the salt water over the cucumbers to completely cover. Open the probiotics and empty them in the water and mix well.

Pour the remaining salt water in a one-gallon zip-top bag sealed to be a weight on top of the pickles. Then place this bag on top of the pickles, making sure they are all submerged in the brine, or place a weight on top, cover and set in a cool place.

The pickles should be ready in 3-7 days. Check daily and skim off any scum. The water and the pickles should taste sour. When they are ready, refrigerate in jars with some juice. Save the remainder of juice for fermenting other vegetables. The brine will become cloudy from the lactic bacteria and sometimes white chunks of colonized bacteria and may be skimmed off.

Contributed by Jackie Graff (sproutrawfood.org)

WHAT ARE PICKLING SPICES?

Pickling spices have peppercorns, bay leaves juniper berries, hot chili pepper and celery seed, and more. These are available everywhere where spices are sold.

PICKLES   65

Sweet Pickle Relish

This is a great condiment to serve with burgers and sandwiches.

Makes 1 quart relish

1 pound small pickling cucumbers, sliced ¼ inch thick
1 red onion, thinly sliced
¾ cup lemon juice
½ cup coconut sugar
1 tsp garlic purée
1 tsp brown mustard seed
1 tsp pickling spices, ground slightly in a spice grinder

Put the lemon juice, coconut sugar, garlic, mustard seeds, and pickling spice in a half gallon jar and mix well. Add the sliced cucumbers and red onions and put the lid on the jar. Shake well to incorporate. Allow the mixture to rest in a cool, dark place for 8-12 hours, or overnight.

Drain the mixture through a colander and reserve the liquid. Put the drained cucumber pickle mixture in a food processor and pulse to create a minced relish texture. Add a little of the reserved liquid to create the desired amount of juiciness. Will keep in a glass jar for up to 2 weeks.

Contributed by Cherie Soria (rawfoodchef.com)

. . . .

Crunchy Pickles (not vegan)

2 tbsp whey *(not vegan)* or ¼ tsp probiotic powder *(vegan)*
Upwards of 5 lb pickling cucumbers
5-6 tannic leaves *(horseradish, oak, grape)*, which will give your pickles the 'crunch'

(optional)
1 handful fresh dill
4-6 dried red chilis
5 garlic cloves, roughly chopped
3 green onions, roughly chopped
¼ cup pickling spices

Brine:
½ gallon of spring water with 6 tbsp sea salt dissolved into it

Equipment:
1 gallon wide-mouthed glass jar *(washed really well)*
Cheesecloth or mesh screen   *(cont...)*

After collecting all your ingredients, wash your cucumbers and prepare them as needed. If you do not have small pickling cucumbers, you may use a larger size, but may need to cut them down in size. You can coin cut larger cukes or cut them into 3-4 inch spears. Do as you wish. Pack the cucumbers into the glass jar to fill it 3/4 full. Add to the brine your tannic leaves, any spices and as many different garden herbs as you wish.

Pour in the brine to cover the cucumbers by at least 1 inch. Stir in your whey or probiotics. Cover the jar with cheese cloth.

Allow to stand at room temperature for 3 days. Keep an eye on the cucumbers and give them an occasional push below the surface of the brine. Taste and check for texture and taste.

Continue to let stand for a 2 days, then taste. Once desired taste is achieved, place in the fridge. Pickles will continue to ferment, slowly, and build flavor over time. Save some of the brine to inoculate your new batch of pickles.

Contributed by Frank Giglio (frankgiglio.com or franksfinestllc.com)

Frank Giglio is a classically trained chef from the New England Culinary Institute in Montpelier, VT, a graduate of The Institute for Integrative Nutrition in NYC and worked under the guidance of Dr. Gabriel Cousens at the Tree Of Life Rejuvenation Center in Patagonia, AZ. With a strong passion for using food as medicine Frank works greatly to produce sustainable cuisine, which to him, means seeking the highest quality foods grown locally and in alignment with the environment.

· · · · · · ·

Pickled Antipasto

Turn garden fresh veggies into a quick base for pasta AND garden salads. Toss our pickled antipasto with dressed lettuce or add to pasta with a splash of oil to make a main course dish.

makes 2 quarts (1.9 l)

Plan on 2 lb total for your mix of vegetables
12 oz. green tomatoes or tomatillos, chopped
12 oz. snap beans, trimmed, steamed 3 minutes
2 cups onion, chopped
1 tbsp garlic, sliced
1 cup olives, coarsely chopped
1 cup ¼ inch-thick rounds banana peppers or other type
½ cup thin strips dried tomatoes *(or dried sweet peppers)*
2 tsp Italian seasoning or other spice combos of choice
4 cups filtered water
2 tbsp unrefined sea salt   *(cont...)*

PICKLES

Soak and trim green beans, then steam for 3 minutes and shock with cold water.

Prep veggies and toss in a large bowl.

Add spices to a clean 2-quart jar and load the mixture, tamping lightly as you go.

Dissolve 2 scant tbsp unrefined sea salt with 4 cups filtered water. Pour over vegetables and keep veggies submerged for 4 days at close to 70 degrees. Refrigerate after fermentation is complete.

After fermentation drizzle with olive oil. On occasion add fresh, chopped Mediterranean herbs, jarred capers, and a squeeze of lemon juice. Toss with pasta, or dressed salad greens, or as a topper for cooked grains.

Contributed by Wendy Valley
(perfectpickler.com)

Wendy Valley's greatest passion rests in the Perfect Pickler Company, which she co-owns with company founder, Bill Hettig. With their canning jar fermentor, The Perfect Pickler, you make your own rich probiotic pickles for pennies in just 4 days!

HELPFUL TIP:

You can make a great Italian vinaigrette salad dressing from this brine. Just mix brine with high quality olive oil, a squeeze of lemon juice, and ground pepper.

WHAT ARE TOMATILLOS?

Tomatillos are members of the tomato family. Find in ethnic and larger supermarkets.

KEFIR

Kefir means "feel good" in Turkish. Easy and fun to make at home*, it is superior to any commercial products. Adding kefir grains or water to a sauce will extend the life of that sauce up to several weeks and months! An absolute must after antibiotic use, kefir also has proven anti-cancer and strong immune-boosting properties. When consumed frequently, it boosts your ability to digest all your foods more efficiently. As a fermented food, kefir increases the vitamin content of the foods fermented with it. *Non-vegan kefirs are denoted in the recipe title.

Cultured Tips!
KEFIR 101

What's is Vegan Kefir (vs. Dairy Kefir)?

Often called water kefir, the grains are not grains at all! They are a SCOBY – Symbiotic Culture of Bacteria and Yeasts. Live kefir grains look like translucent pebbles.

These grains eat the sugar in a food, leaving behind a more nutritious dish because of the lactic acid and beneficial bacteria it adds.

Kefir is an ancient cultured food rich in amino acids, enzymes, calcium, magnesium, phosphorus and B vitamins. It is typically a dairy product, but dairy kefir grains are different. Water kefir grains are vegan, and we have figured out innovative ways to use water-kefir grains to pickle and ferment so many things including soda, yogurt, pickles, ketchup, mustard salsa and more.

Vegan kefir grains come in two types: Pure live grains and powdered culture starter. (The powdered culture starter uses natural dextrose as a carrier that is consumed during the process of fermentation).

What is the Difference between Live Grains and Kefir Culture Starter?

The most noticeable difference is the live grains can be used for a lifetime. Powdered kefir grains can be used up to about 7 times before you need to discard them.

Live grains come wet if you purchase them or get them from a friend. Sometimes you can also buy them dry (dehydrated) and then you add water to them at home to get them wet and living again. Live kefir grains grow and multiply as you use them. Therefore, the make a great gift for your ferment-curious friends. Live grains can be eaten, though usually they are removed from your dish before you eat it so you can reuse the grains. Pets and babies love food that is fermented from kefir, and even the grains themselves.

Kefir culture starter is a product created by the company Body Ecology. You use one envelope of kefir starter to begin (see below). From there, ¼ cup of a previous batch will ferment 1 quart of liquid up to 7 times more. After 7 times, you discard the starter and begin again with a new envelope.

Getting Started with Kefir Grains

If your grains are wet, you don't need to do anything special to them. Just follow a recipe to make what you like.

KEFIR

If your grains came to you dry, soak them in warm water for a few hours. They will plump up and be ready to use.

When you are not using your grains, you can keep them in a bottle with water in the fridge. They will sit in this "hotel" until you use them again or give them away. Alternatively, you can dehydrate the grains and store them in a glass container.

Getting Started with Body Ecology Kefir Starter

For initial usage, mix together the entire contents of one foil package of kefir starter and one quart of slightly warmed coconut water or water sweetened with sugar into a container (preferably glass). The warmth of the water should be about skin temperature, or 92 degrees.

Shake, stir or whip with a whisk to mix well. Put a lid on the container. Let this mixture ferment 24-48 hours on the counter. Refrigerate the mixture afterwards.

Then drink this kefir water or use it in any recipe you like. If you don't use coconut water, you can make kefir water using water sweetened with sugar and dried fruit. See the resources below to get specific recipe ideas. Remember that regardless of which culture you have, even in your refrigerator the fermentation process continues. Chilling simply slows down the fermentation process.

How Do I Use Kefir?

You will find recipes all over the internet and in books. My favorite resources include: My "Focus on Fermentation" classes, *Nourishing Traditions* by Sally Fallon and the website NourishedKitchen.com.

- Soda: The most basic way to use kefir grains. The natural fermentation process using kefir grains makes excellent natural ginger ale, root beer, lemonade, oringina and more.
- Yogurt: I will teach you how in my "Focus on Fermentation" classes. You can also find a recipe and video demonstration at my website rawbayarea.com
- Savories: Sauerkraut and other pickled vegetables including cucumbers, grape leaves, turnips, lemons, jalapeños and more!
- Condiments: Salsa, Ketchup, Mustard, Chutney, Horseradish, Jam and much more.

You can substitute an equal amount of live kefir grains or kefir water in any recipe that calls for whey. You can also add kefir to most fermenting recipes, even if it doesn't call for any starter at all. In this case, the kefir grains will simply make the fermenting process go a little more smoothly.

Where Can I Find Kefir Grains?

- Come to my classes, I carry both types of kefir.
- On-line sources for live grains include: Yemoos, Zoe the Kefir Mom and Marilyn the Kefir Lady.
- Find your Body Ecology kefir starter on-line at renegadehealth.com.

Anything Else I Should Know about Kefir?

You will know that you are doing things right with your kefir grains when they start to grow bigger and multiply – and you are happy with the result of your fermented item. If any mold ever appears, you should discard your batch and start again.

Kefir grains usually do their fermenting within 2 days – 1 week, which means you will need to use them in a new batch of ingredients frequently. You may find that you don't want to keep up with this rapid schedule. Live kefir grains will slow down their growth, and survive, in the refrigerator. They also can be dehydrated and kept in a glass container.

If you are the type of person who does not like to tend cultures, Body Ecology's Starter may be a nice option. After 8 generations you can take a complete break. Whereas, live culture grains can be used for life. If you want to make things with kefir, but don't have grains or starter, play with using water and probiotic powder. Sometimes that works well. Alternatively, veggie culture starter can sometimes work well in some recipes.

If you have live culture you don't want anymore, or more grains than you can use, please get in touch with me. Likely, I can give them to other students.

Contributed by Heather Haxo Phillips (rawbayarea.com)

Heather Haxo Phillips is the Principal and Founder of Raw Bay Area. Through Raw Bay Area, Heather offers raw food coaching, classes and special events to inspire and educate people about the power of raw food. Heather is a certified raw food chef/instructor and graduate of the Living Light Culinary Arts Institute.

· · · · · · ·

Classic Vegan Water Kefir

3 cups water
3-4 tbsp kefir grains (or 1 packet Body Ecology kefir starter)
2 tbsp organic white sugar
1 tbsp organic succanat or another brown unrefined sugar such as maple syrup
1 dried apricots
1 dried fig
1 lemon wedge

Place all the ingredients in a jar. Put a mesh lid on the jar. Allow it to sit in a warm place (65-80 degrees) for 8-48 hours. Kefir is ready when it is slightly effervescent, tastes slightly sour, and is slightly viscous. Strain off the grains and the fruit. Finished kefir can be stored in the refrigerator and will last for weeks. It will continue to ferment, but at a much slower rate.

Contributed by Heather Haxo Phillips (rawbayarea.com)

KEFIR

SEE HOW TO MAKE COCONUT WATER KEFIR:
RENEGADEHEALTH.COM/CULTURED/KEFIR

Vegan Coconut Kefir

Makes 4 cups

Approximately 2 tbsp fresh kefir grains or a packet of vegan kefir starter
Approximately 3 cups coconut water

Begin with room temperature coconut water. If the water is cold, heat it very briefly in a saucepan until it becomes warm (not hot) to the touch.

If you are using a packet of dry vegan kefir starter (available from Body Ecology) place the coconut water and kefir starter in a blender and process briefly. Transfer the liquid to a glass jar. If you are using fresh grains, put the grains and the coconut water together in a glass jar without blending. Put a lid on the jar.

Allow it to sit in a warm place (65-80 degrees F) for 8-48 hours. Kefir is ready when it is slightly effervescent, tastes slightly sour, and is slightly viscous. Finished kefir can be stored in the refrigerator and will last for weeks. It will continue to ferment, but at a much slower rate.

Contributed by Heather Haxo Phillips (rawbayarea.com)

HELPFUL TIP:

Vegan kefir is just one use for kefir grains. You can make many soda variations using sweet water instead of coconut water. You can also use the grains to ferment all kinds of vegetables and condiments. For more info and kefir variations, check out the kefir recipe and handout at www.rawbayarea.com.

WHAT IS E3 LIVE?

You may have heard about the wonderful, detoxifying effects of Blue-Green Algae. Unlike many blue-green algae supplements that come in pill form, however, E3 Live is a live, liquid, non-GMO blue-green algae supplement that is harvested from Klamath Lake in Oregon, one of the most nutrient rich water deposits in the world. You can order some at renegadehealth.com/e3live

HELPFUL TIP:

Coconut kefir can be blended with any type of frozen fruit in the blender to make a refreshing and healthy sorbet, great for kids and adults!

Green-Ya Coladas

½ cup coconut kefir *(see page 73)*
1-2 shots E3 Live algae *(1 for each person drinking; I always like to share)*
1 cup fermented coconut milk *(see Coconut yogurt page 78)*
2 cups frozen pineapple
A bit of water
Squeeze of lime, pinch of vanilla, few sprigs of mint or dazzle of your choice *(optional)*

Blend pineapple and water in blender until smooth. Add in E3 Live and blend for a few seconds. Add in coconut milk and blend a bit more.

Pour into cold glasses and stir in coconut kefir.

Contributed by Gina LaVerde
(blissedlife.com)

Strawberry Nectarine Kefir Sorbet

1 and ½ cups frozen strawberries
½ cup young coconut kefir or coconut yogurt *(see page 73 or 78)*
½ a nectarine
1 pinch white stevia powder
Seeds from 1 vanilla bean *(optional)*

Blend all ingredients in a high speed blender using a tamper. Blend less for a sorbet, blend more for a shake. Garnish with chopped fresh fruit. For fun and extra nutrition, you can sprinkle bee pollen or wheat germ, and drizzle with blackstrap molasses for a healthy 'sundae'. Enjoy!

Contributed by Cecilia Kinzie
(rawglow.com)

Dairy Kefir (not vegan)

Making kefir is easy and much more affordable than buying it. You can use any type of milk except ultra-pasteurized milk. This is a really dead food - you cannot make culture with it. My first choice would be organic, then raw, then goat, then cow, then pasteurized but NOT homogenized. The most digestible would be organic, raw goat milk. Choose the option that works best for your situation.

Milk *(see amount below)*
1 tsp kefir grains
1-liter pickl-it jar
Water for airlock

Take a teaspoon of kefir grains (with milk if they are being stored in milk - no need to strain them) and place into your pickl-it jar. Add the milk until it reaches the shoulder of the jar.

Close the jar and add the airlock with water. Place the jar either in a cupboard or wrap a towel around it. The lactic acid bacteria thrive in darkness. Leave kefir at room temperature - when the kefir has thickened and tastes tangy to your liking, it is finished.

Kefir generally takes 12-48 hours to form. The exact amount of time will vary depending on environmental factors, the most important of which is temperature. Cold retards the fermentation process, so kefir will form more slowly in a cold area (and can be all but stopped by placing the grains in milk in the refrigerator). Heat speeds the process, so kefir will form more quickly in a warm area and will be more likely to over-culture. I recommend standard room temperature whenever possible. Allowing the kefir grains to remain in milk longer than 48 hours risks starving the kefir grains and potentially damaging them.

Strain the kefir grains from the milk - your kefir is ready to drink or use in a recipe. Place the grains in a new batch of milk and restart the process.

Contributed by Lisa Herndon (lisascounterculture.com)

Lisa Herndon is quite passionate about "real food" and loves being able to share her recipes and techniques for creating nourishing and traditional foods. Lisa's Counter Culture offers focused hands-on workshops, which give you a chance to become more familiar and comfortable with the overall process when you start fermenting or cooking at home.

Cultured Tips!

CARING FOR DAIRY KEFIR GRAINS

Should I Rinse the Grains?

I do not recommend rinsing the grains between batches unless they stop making kefir effectively (which can sometimes be attributed to a build up of yeast on the grains).

If it becomes necessary to rinse the grains, use filtered water if possible to avoid chemical exposure.

Should I Stir or Shake the Kefir While it is Fermenting?

I sometimes do this to see how it is progressing - but is not necessary for making kefir.

How Do I Slow the Fermentation Process?

Put the kefir grains in the fresh milk, place a tight lid on the container and place it in the refrigerator. The cold will greatly retard the culturing process, and they can keep this way for up to several weeks.

If at the end of that period you require more time, simply repeat the process with fresh milk.

How Do I Keep Other Ferments from Cross Contamination?

When items are being actively cultured (and don't have lids), I suggest keeping a distance of at least several feet (and preferably more) between items. So, if you have kombucha or sourdough going - keep them away from the kefir - since these are usually open to the air.

When your cultured items are being stored in the refrigerator with tight fitting lids, there is no need to keep distance between them.

What if My Kefir has Separated into Curds and Whey?

Kefir will separate if it over-cultures a bit. To prevent this from happening in the future, simply reduce the amount of time you allow the kefir to culture or reduce the temperature at which it is culturing (i.e. move it to a cooler area of the house). I usually just stir it a bit and than proceed; if it tastes too sour, you may want to add some fruit to sweeten it.

Contributed by Lisa Herndon (lisascounterculture.com)

YOGURT

You can use more than milk to make yogurt! In this section, we'll show you how to use cashews, coconut meat, almonds, and more to make delicious homemade yogurts*.

Here's a helpful tip when creating your own yogurts: Don't expect your yogurt to be as thick as store bought products. These are often thickened with additives.
*Non-vegan yogurts are denoted in the recipe title.

78   CULTURED: HOW TO MAKE HEALTHY FERMENTED FOODS AT HOME

Vanilla Coconut Yogurt

Makes 3 cups

2 cups young coconut meat *(about 2-3 coconuts)*
¼ cup kefir, or 2 probiotic pills
1 pinch vanilla bean powder or the seeds from inside ½ of a vanilla bean

Blend the coconut and coconut water/probiotic in a blender until completely smooth and slightly warm. Add the vanilla powder and pulse it into the mixture. Place the coconut cream in a jar and put on lid. Allow to culture on the counter at 65-80 degrees (on top of a warm dehydrator is ideal) for 8-12 hours. It will expand, so make sure there is room for that in your jar. The yogurt is ready when it gets spongy and slightly sour. Store in the refrigerator for up to one week. It will continue to ferment and sour in the fridge.

Contributed by Heather Haxo Phillips (rawbayarea.com)

RAW OR NOT?

It's up to you to decide if you'd like to make yogurt with raw milk. If you're making it raw, be sure you get fresh milk. You can also boil the raw milk at home first, then allow it to cool to 90-100 degrees before starting the recipe. This pasteurization process will deactivate some of the enzymes, but the fermentation process will create a combination of healthy benefits that may be different, but still beneficial.

SERVING IDEAS:

Serve your yogurt in a bowl with fresh fruit, or make a fruit yogurt by blending ½ cup fresh fruit into the yogurt and top with honey, if desired. You could also make a beautiful parfait, by putting the yogurt in wine glass with layers of fresh strawberry jam (see page 81). Top it with your favorite granola or chopped nuts.

WHAT IS A YOUNG COCONUT?

Unlike the hairy, aged brown coconuts you're used to seeing in the supermarket, young coconuts often appear with their green outer shell or white inner skin still intact. These younger coconuts contain more minerals and health benefits than when they age.

HOW DO YOU OPEN THE COCONUT?

Coconuts can be opened by shaving off their outer layers with a sharp kitchen knife until you reach the inner core or 'nut.' Next, you crack the edges of the nut's peak until it is able to be pried open, revealing the tasty and nutritious coconut water and flesh inside.

VISIT RENEGADEHEALTH.COM/CULTURED/OPEN TO SEE HOW TO OPEN A YOUNG COCONUT & RENEGADEHEALTH.COM/CULTURED/YOGURT TO LEARN HOW TO MAKE COCONUT YOGURT

Strawberry Jam

1 ½ cups strawberries or raspberries, fresh or frozen
½ cup soaked dates or date paste

Place berries and dates into a blender. Blend until very smooth. Taste the jam. If it is not sweet enough, add a few drops of stevia or more date paste. If you want it thicker, add a tablespoon of ground chia or psyllium husk.

Stored in a glass container, the jam will keep for up to 5 days.

Contributed by Heather Haxo Phillips (rawbayarea.com)

Almond Yogurt

2 cups organic raw almonds, soaked for 12 hours
¼ cup Real Food. Real Life. Grapefruit flavor Pro-Belly-Otic*, or ¼ cup coconut kefir
¼ cup all natural sweetener like Lokanto, organic erythritol or xylitol *(Lokanto, organic erythritol and xylitol made from birch are great options that do not feed candida yeast.)*
1 tbsp cinnamon
1 tbsp vanilla extract
1/4 tsp sea salt

*Pro-Belly-Otic is a probiotic liquid with extra hardy probiotic strains, which you can get from realfoodreallife.tv. If you don't have this product, you can use a vegetable starter or coconut kefir.

Soak almonds for 12 hours (To soak, cover with water and leave out in a covered glass container. This removes the anti-nutrients in nuts and seeds that makes them difficult to digest). After soaking, drain water from the almonds and rinse.

To ferment the almonds, put the almonds into a food processor (with the 'S blade') or high speed blender and blend until smooth. If you have a Vitamix, Blendtec or other high speed blender, you can often get a more "whipped" consistency, which can be nice, but is not necessary. *(cont...)*

80 CULTURED: HOW TO MAKE HEALTHY FERMENTED FOODS AT HOME

Add in the Pro-Belly-Otic and blend it in. Some fermented nut recipes use Rejuvelac, which may be problematic for people with candida yeast issues. I prefer to have a very medicinal-end product that is full of hardy probiotics; so, I like whole food probiotic sources.

Let this mixture sit in a covered, air tight glass container for 24 hours. You can leave it on your countertop (do not refrigerate). This will allow the almonds to ferment.

After 24 hours, pour the mixture back into your blender or food processor or blender. Taste it to see if you like the plain almond yogurt. I prefer to add some flavoring and if you do too, add the natural sweetener, coconut oil, cinnamon, sea salt and vanilla and blend up. Taste and see if you need to add anything else. Make sure you like the taste before continuing with the recipe. Everyone's tastes are a bit different.

Add your favorite berries for a breakfast treat!t

Contributed by Heather Fougnier (nowradianthealth.com)

• • • • • • •

Cashew Yogurt

Makes 3 cups, or 12 servings

Nutrition Note: Cashew Yogurt is nut based, so with 10 grams of fat per 1/4-cup serving, remember to keep your serving sizes moderate.

2 cups cashews*, soaked for 2–4 hours, rinsed, and drained
1 ½ cups purified water
¼ tsp probiotic powder

Combine the cashews, water, and probiotic powder in a blender, and process until smooth and creamy. Add more water, if needed, to achieve a smooth texture.

Pour the thick cream into a 1-quart glass jar and cover the top with cheesecloth. Place it in a warm location (65-85 degrees) to ferment for 8-12 hours, or until it has fermented to suit your taste. (Less fermentation time is required in warmer weather.) Stored in a sealed glass container in the refrigerator. Cashew Yogurt will keep for up to 1 week.

* Other nuts and seeds may also be used to make yogurt, including macadamia nuts, peeled almonds, and sunflower seeds.

Contributed by Cherie Soria (rawfoodchef.com)

BeLive's Almond Coconut Yogurt

1 cup raw almonds (soaked 12-24 hours, rinsed)
1 ½ cups coconut water
1 ½ cups coconut meat
½ tsp NCP (Natural Choice Product) probiotic blend powder, or your favorite starter culture.

Blend until creamy and place in bowl. Then, let it sit at room temperature for 3-5 hours (depending on temperature of the room), until it is cultured and has a bite to it. Use immediately or place in sealed container and refrigerate. It will last up to 1 week.

You can use this as a creamy base to many dressings, sauces and soups.

Contributed by Brian James Lucas, aka Chef BeLive (chefbelive.com)

Brian James Lucas (Chef BeLive) is one of the pioneers of the 90s gourmet raw food movement. He considers himself a "transitional" gourmet raw chef, specializing in creating raw living cuisine that tastes superb thereby helping make people's first experience with raw living foods equal to many of their cooked favorites.

• • • • • • •

Yogurt (not vegan)

When Kevin was experiencing problems with candida, he started to use a little goat's milk yogurt as a therapeutic food. He and I learned how to make our own... this is how we did it!

1 quart organic goat's milk
2 tbsp coconut sugar *(or another sweetener like honey, maple syrup or coconut syrup)*
1 packet Body Ecology culture starter *(or your favorite culture starter)*

Heat milk to 90 degrees and add the sweetener. Slowly mix in culture starter.

Place mix in yogurt maker containers; I like to use the Yolife yogurt maker, which you can get at renegadehealth.com/yolife.

Turn on yogurt maker and let ferment 8-12 hours. (You can also use a dehydrator set at about 90 degrees.) Once fermented place in the refrigerator.

When ready to serve, add fruit, honey, cinnamon, and vanilla powder for a nice yummy breakfast or treat. Or, eat plain. Unsweetened, it could double as sour cream and could be served with a nice raw burrito.

Contributed by Annmarie Gianni (renegadehealth.com)

CHEESE & SOUR CREAM

This section contains a selection of vegan and non-vegan cheeses* that you can make at home. Be sure to experiment and have fun with the seasonings to put your own personal touches to these recipes. *Non-vegan cheeses are denoted in the recipe title.

Basic Nut Cheese

Makes 2 cups, or 8 servings

2 cups almonds *(peeled)*, cashews, macadamia
nuts, or hazelnuts *(see notes)*
1 cup purified water
½ tsp probiotic powder

Combine the nuts, water, and probiotic powder
in a blender and process until smooth. Add a
small amount of additional water, if necessary, to
facilitate processing. However, use as little water
as possible to achieve a thick, creamy consistency.

Select a pint-size (500 mL), or larger, strainer (a
plastic berry basket works well) and line it with
cheesecloth, allowing several inches of the cloth
to drape down around the sides. Set the strainer
on top of a shallow baking dish and pour the
nut batter into the cheesecloth. The baking dish
will catch the liquid as it drains from the cheese.
Fold the excess cheesecloth over the top of the
cheese, and place the bundle in a warm (65-85
degrees) location to ferment for 8-12 hours. (Less
fermentation time is required in warmer weather.)

After about 2 hours of fermenting, place a weight
(such as a cup of grain or seeds) on top of the
cheese to press out the excess liquid.

After the cheese has fermented to suit your taste,
use it in any recipe calling for nut cheese. Stored
in a sealed glass container in the refrigerator, Basic
Nut Cheese will keep for up to 1 week.

Contributed by Cherie Soria
(rawfoodchef.com)

VARIATIONS:

Almond or Hazelnut Cheese:
Soak whole raw almonds in
nearly boiling purified water for
5 minutes, drain, and remove
the skins using your fingers.
Immediately plunge the skinned
almonds into cold water and
soak them for 8-12 hours. Rinse,
drain, and blend as directed.
Macadamia Nut Cheese: Use
unsoaked nuts if you have a
high-performance blender. Or,
soak nuts for 6 hours, rinse, and
drain. Blend as directed.
Cashew Cheese: Use
unsoaked nuts if you have a
high-performance blender.
Or, soak cashews or pine nuts
for 2 hours, then rinse, drain,
and blend. No cheesecloth is
required, since these nuts will
not release any liquid during
fermentation. Pour the mixture
into a bowl (rather than a
strainer) for step 2.

HELPFUL TIPS:

Remember that nuts are high in
fat and calories, so it's important that these cheeses be used
in moderation. Per serving,
Almond Cheese delivers almost
80% of the RDA for vitamin E
and over 100 mg of calcium,
Cashew Cheese supplies 33%
of the RDA for zinc, and Macadamia Cheese offers over 75%
of the RDA for manganese.

CHEESE & SOUR CREAM (VEGAN & NON VEGAN)   85

Italian Pesto Almond Torte

Makes one 2-cup torte, or 6 servings

Seasoned Almond Cheese:
1 cup almonds, hot soaked for 5 min. & peeled,
then soaked in cold water to cover for 8-12 hours.
½ cup *(or less)* purified water
1 tbsp light miso
1 tsp nutritional yeast
Pinch of nutmeg
Pinch of Himalayan crystal salt

Blend all of the ingredients in a high-powered
blender until creamy, adding as little water as
possible. Pour the mixture into a cheesecloth-
lined strainer on top of a shallow baking dish, and
ferment it according to the instructions for Basic
Nut Cheese (see page 84).

When the fermentation time is completed, remove
the cheesecloth and place the cheese in a tightly
covered container. Refrigerate until needed.

Basil Pesto:
2 cups fresh basil leaves, tightly packed
¼ cup pine nuts
1 tbsp olive oil
1 tbsp flax oil
½ tsp crushed garlic
¼ tsp Himalayan crystal salt

Place all of the ingredients in a food processor
outfitted with the "S" blade and purée, leaving the
mixture a little bit chunky. If possible, chill for an
hour or more before assembling the torte.

To assemble the torte, drape a 2-3-cup mold with
damp cheesecloth. Evenly pack a third of the cheese
into the bottom of the mold. Next, layer half of
the pesto into the mold. Firmly pack the pesto into
place. Evenly pack another one-third portion of the

(cont...)

WHAT IS MISO?

Miso is a Japanese cooking
paste that is traditional made
from fermented soybeans. It
is used as a base for many
soups, seasonings and
spreads. It aids in digestion,
helps to lower cholesterol
and strengthens the immune
system. (See page 94 for a
Miso recipe.)

WHAT IS NUTRITIONAL YEAST?

Nutritional yeast is essentially
deactivated, fermented
yeast. No longer a baking
ingredient, this yeast has a
nutty, cheesy taste that can
add flavor to many dishes.
Favored by many vegans
as a food seasoning, it also
contains several amino acids
and b vitamins.

cheese on top of the pesto. Gently and firmly place the remaining pesto on top of the cheese. Firmly pack the pesto into place. Spread the remaining cheese on top of the pesto, and press firmly and smoothly into place. Time permitting, chill for 1 hour.

To serve fold the cheesecloth back to expose the cheese, and invert the serving plate on top of the torte-filled mold. Center the plate carefully. Holding the plate and the torte together, turn the plate over and remove the cheesecloth and the mold, exposing the beautiful torte, now centered on the serving plate. Arrange crudités or crackers around the sides of the plate. Store in an airtight container in the refrigerator for four to five days.

Contributed by Cherie Soria (rawfoodchef.com)

• • • • • • •

Herbed Cheese Spread

Makes 1 cup, or 4 to 6 servings

1 cup Seasoned Almond Cheese *(see recipe for Italian Pesto Almond Torte, page85)*
1 tbsp pine nuts, chopped
1 tbsp red onion, finely minced
½ tbsp fresh parsley, minced
1 tsp fresh dill weed, minced
½ tsp green onion, finely minced
¼ tsp garlic, puréed
Pinch of pepper

Combine all of the ingredients in a medium bowl, and stir well. Store in an airtight container in the refrigerator for up to four days.

Contributed by Cherie Soria (rawfoodchef.com)

HELPFUL TIP:

For a delicious savory cheese sauce, blend the cheese mixture in a high-powered blender until smooth. For a chili cheese sauce for Mexican cuisine, add Mexican chili powder blend and paprika.

CHEESE & SOUR CREAM (VEGAN & NON VEGAN)   87

Herbed Almond 'Chèvre'

Makes 2 cups

2 cups almonds
1 cup Rejuvelac *(see page 100)* or vegan kefir *(see page 72)*
½ tsp salt
1 tbsp lemon juice
1 tbsp miso
Pinch of nutmeg
Dried or fresh herbs and spices to garnish, such as basil, parsley, rosemary or cracked pepper

Blanch the almonds by bringing approximately 4 cups water almost to a boil then turning off the heat. Add the almonds and allow to sit for 3-5 minutes. Drain and rinse the almonds in cool water, then slip off the peels. Place the almonds and Rejuvelac in a high-speed blender and process until smooth, adding more Rejuvelac if necessary to form a smooth, creamy texture.

Pour the mixture into a nut milk bag or cheesecloth-lined strainer. Allow to strain and ferment for 12-36 hours, until desired tartness is achieved. Remove the cheese from the strainer and add the salt, lemon juice, miso and nutmeg.

To create a typical chevre-style log, place your cheese as a ball in the middle of a large piece of wax paper. Roll the sides of the wax paper until you have created a tube shape with your cheese. Place your cheese, in its wax paper, in the refrigerator 8-24 hours so that it can set and thicken. Just before serving, sprinkle the herbs/spices on all sides of the roll until well covered. Then roll it off the wax paper and onto a plate. Cut and serve as desired. To mold the cheese into a thick chevre-round, place a nutmilk bag or cheesecloth over your favorite round mold. Firmly push the cheese into the mold. Refrigerate the cheese until ready to use, 8-24 hours is best. Plate it by turning over the mold and removing your cheesecloth. Decorate with your herbs and spices. Stored in an airtight container in the refrigerator, the 'Chevre' will last for up to one week.

Contributed by Heather Haxo Phillips (rawbayarea.com)

HELPFUL TIPS:

For a cheese with even fewer steps, use raw cashews or macadamias instead of almonds. They don't need to be peeled though soaking them for 20 min-4 hours will make them soft and easier to blend.

Most almonds and cashews are labeled as raw when they have, in fact, been pasteurized or heated. For the most nutritious nut, buy your raw almonds directly from the farmer at farmer's markets (If you are California). You can also find truly raw almonds at renegadehealth.com/almonds.

- SEE HOW TO MAKE A NO-DAIRY CHEESE: RENEGADEHEALTH.COM/CULTURED/SOFTCHEESE
- LEARN HOW TO MAKE HARD RAW VEGAN CHEESE: RENEGADEHEALTH.COM/CULTURED/HARDCHEESE
- LEARN HOW TO MAKE A VEGAN 'CHÈVRE': RENEGADEHEALTH.COM/CULTURED/HERBCHEESE

Cultured Cheese

2 cups raw cashews *(soaked for 4 hours, rinsed well)*
½ tbsp Proteolytic Probiotics *(Natural Choice Product)* OR ¼ cup rejuvelac *(see page 100)*
1/3 cup water *(spring, structured or filtered water)*
1 ¾ tsp salt *(Himilayan, Celtic or Sea)*

Process or blend cashews and probiotics well and place in a bowl.

If using probiotics, leave uncovered at room temperature (between 70-85 degrees) for 6-8 hours. If it is warmer temperature, leave for for less time.

If using rejuvelac, leave uncovered at same room temperature for 12-15 hours, or longer if warmer - checking it for a bite. The advantage to using a "Probiotic Powder" is it predigests the truly raw cashew nuts into essential amino acids, fatty acids and glucose, making it bioavailable.

Contributed by Brian James Lucas aka Chef BeLive (chefbelive.com)

Mini Raw Ravioli

Makes 2 servings

Sauce:
1 cup tomatoes
¼ cup green onions
¼ tsp dried thyme
¼ tsp dried onion, minced
¼ tsp dried rosemary
½ tsp dried basil
1 ½ tsp cold pressed mild olive oil
2 tsp maple syrup or 4 soaked medjool dates
½ tsp salt (Himilayan, Celtic or Sea Salt)

CHEESE & SOUR CREAM (VEGAN & NON VEGAN)

Blend Well.

Make cultured cheese from Cultured Cheese recipe. (see page 88)

Ravioli:
For the ravioli noodle, choose zucchini or watermelon daikon radish. Use a vegetable peeler or mandoline to create round slices, as thin as possible.

Place cultured cheese inside zucchini and fold into half moons, shape of ravioli. After finished place on serving plates and add sauce on top.

Contributed by Brian James Lucas aka Chef BeLive (chefbelive.com)

• • • • • • •

BeLive's Cashew Sour Cream

1 ½ cups raw cashews *(soaked 2-4 hrs, then rinsed)*
1 ½ cups coconut meat
1 tbsp lemon juice
¾ cups water
1 ⅛ tsp salt of choice
½ tsp NCP Probiotic Blend Power *(Natural Choice Product),* or your favorite probiotic starter

Blend all ingredients until creamy, then place in a bowl and let sit at room temperature for 3-5 hours (depending on temperature of room) until it has a bite and is cultured.

Use immediately or place in sealed container and refrigerate. It will last up to 1 week. You can use this in Mexican food, and it goes great on sandwiches too.

Contributed by Brian James Lucas aka Chef BeLive (chefbelive.com)

• • • • • • •

Curd-Cheese & Fermented Whey (not vegan)

You can use this curd cheese exactly as you would use chevre or cottage cheese.

1 gallon organic milk, any fat content from 1% to full will work. This recipe calls for pasteurized milk and has not been tested starting with raw milk.
2 tbsp organic plain yogurt, any fat content will work because we're just using it as a starter culture.

Time required for production of fermented whey and curd cheese:
Fermentation time: 10-14 hours (less in warmer temps). *(cont...)*

90   CULTURED: HOW TO MAKE HEALTHY FERMENTED FOODS AT HOME

Time in front of the stove: 15-20 minutes, once before fermentation and once after.
Cheese drying time: 3 hours.
Cooking time: Zero! You are not heating above 103-6 degrees.

Equipment required:
2 large pots, one slightly larger to use as a makeshift double boiler (the inner pot, the one you pour
    the milk into, should be stainless steel; milk will stick to aluminum, glass, or ceramic
Nut milk bag or linen cloth for straining, 24 inch square or slightly larger (cheesecloth has
    holes that are too large)

Pour 1 gallon milk into the smaller of your two large pots. Place this pot into the second pot
so that the water level is about halfway up the side of the smaller pot.

Turn heat to high, and heat until the milk is body temperature, stirring occasionally to equalize
the temp. Check temperature by inserting clean spoon and sipping the milk. Do not use your
finger because that will introduce unwanted bacteria.

Once the temperature is correct, place about ½ cup of the warmed milk into a large glass and
stir together with the 2 tbsp yogurt until the lumpiness is all gone. Then pour this back into
the warmed milk, stirring well to distribute. Note: You are innoculating the milk with live
bacteria from the yogurt. Cover pot and remove from double boiler setup. If it's cool in your
house, wrap pot in a towel and set aside in a warmish place (70 degrees). Do not disturb the
pot if you can help it, and don't stir.

This is the fermentation phase, which requires 10-14 hours. It takes longer if it's much less
than 70 and shorter if it's warmer. The fermentation phase is temperature sensitive, and I'd
recommend not doing it if it's a hot day and if you can't place the pot somewhere cooler than
78 d egrees. Do not stir, and try not to disturb the pot. You can tell it's done when tiny curds
form. Notice the tiny curds adhering to the pot.

After 10-14 hours, the milk has been converted into a suspension of tiny curds and gives off
a pleasant yogurty smell. Bacterial action has generated acid that coagulated the curds so they
separated out of the milk. At this point, the milk solution is still white. Next, CAREFULLY
lower the fermented milk back into the double boiler setup and place back onto stove. Do
NOT stir. As before, you want a hot flame to get the water boiling. Then, turn it down once
it's going or it will boil over.
Heat the fermented milk to the temperature of a high fever, about 103 degrees. This takes about
15-20 minutes. Again, do not stir. Test by bringing a spoonful of the yellowish whey liquid

WHAT IS A NUT MILK BAG, AND WHERE CAN I GET ONE?
These bags are ideal for any number of straining or sprouting uses. The fine
mesh material minimizes sediment and also allows for sprouting of even the
smallest of seeds and grains. You can find them in most health food stores or
online at renegadehealth.com/nutbag.

CHEESE & SOUR CREAM (VEGAN & NON VEGAN) 91

(not the curds) to your lips. Remember, do not use your finger. What's going on here? You've brewed a giant culture loaded with trillions of bacteria. These bacteria have enzymes that, in the presence of a weak acid, coagulate the casein, precipitating it out of solution. That's why you get those tiny little curds. There's a slight charge on these proteins that attracts them all to each other, and as you heat the pot, the white curds draw together and the separation generates a clearish, light-yellow liquid - the whey - in which the loosely clumped curds are submerged.

Next, gently remove the pot from the double boiler and set aside. Pour the boiling water out of the larger pot and place in the sink. Top with a colander lined with linen Gradually pour the warm curds and whey into the colander, allowing time for it to pass through and avoiding overflow.

Working carefully, gather the linen into a ball, tying opposite ends together in square knots. Hang linen ball over the pot you just emptied to allow the whey to drip out and the curds to come together. This takes about 3 hours. Note" the wire hook shown here was just a wire hanger cut and bent to be exactly the right length for this particular cupboard's handle.

You can dry it faster by spinning the linen as the ball shrinks to apply gentle pressure. The completed cheese has the consistency of chèvre (goat cheese) and in addition to being the perfect consistency for cheese balls, is useful flaked onto salads, as a substitute for cottage cheese, and topped with fruits, savory spices, and/or nuts.

Contributed by Dr. Cate Shanahan (drcate.com)

• • • • • • •

Smokin' Cheese Balls (non vegan)

This recipe was passed on to me from a Ukrainian woman, whose 96-year-old dad still rolls his own cheese balls. They make for a probiotic-packed, low-carb hors d'oeuvres.

1.5 lb curd cheese *(approximate yield from above)*
2 cups shredded smoked Gouda cheese, room temperature
1/2 cup *(1 stick)* unsalted butter, room temperature
2 tbsp whey *(from above, page 89)*
1 tsp Annie's Organic Brand Worchestershire sauce *(without high fructose corn syrup)*
1 tsp Annie's Organic ketchup *(or homemade)*
1 cup raw or toasted pecans or walnuts, chopped
Crustini, or for low-carbers and paleo, use celery spears or cucumber hollows for spreading

Place all ingredients except nuts and crustini/celery in the bowl of an electric mixer fitted with a paddle attachment. Mix until well combined, then place bowl in refrigerator to chill overnight.

When hungry, roll cheese mixture into a ball. Place nuts in a shallow dish. Roll cheese in nuts to fully coat. Serve on your choice of substrate.

Contributed by Dr. Cate Shanahan (drcate.com)

WHAT IS MISO?

Shira Locarni Says...

Miso has been a traditional fermented paste of Asian cultures for thousands of years and is known for its many health promoting properties.

Koji, or Aspergillus oryzae spore, is the B-12 synthesizing organism that is used to ferment miso. The best part about making your own homemade version is that you can use any bean you like. I use garbanzo bean, my all time favorite!

I know the thought of making your own miso can seem intimidating at first, but it's really not that difficult once you get down the basics, it's just a matter of waiting for the end result. You can expand on your homemade recipe with more experience, adding even grains and other beans. But, it is good to begin with a basic, simple recipe to get you started.

MISO & TEMPEH

Fermented soy has been the preferred way to eat this nutritious legume in many cultures for thousands of years. In this section, we'll teach you how to make homemade miso and tempeh at home (soy free)!

Homemade Garbanzo Miso Recipe

5 cups dried garbanzo beans, soaked overnight (traditional soy is used, see side note*)
1 cup sea salt
3 tbsp unpasteurized miso
5 cups koji
1 cup cooking liquid

Equipment:
A one gallon glass jar or a crock of similar size
Plate, lid or wooden disk that fits snugly inside the jar
Heavy weight or clean rock
Thick cotton cloth to cover everything

Cook the beans until soft. Strain and save 1 cup of the cooking liquid. Allow beans to cool and dry in a strainer for an hour or two. Process beans in a food processor for desired texture.

Dissolve ¾ cup sea salt into 1 cup cooking liquid to make a brine. Mash the 3 tbsp unpasteurized miso into 1 cup brine. Mix brine (containing salt and 3 tbsp miso) with the koji.

In a big bowl, add processed beans to this brine mixture. This is your miso.

Packing for Fermentation: (I often do this part first while the garbanzos are cooling.)
Wet the sides of the jar slightly with hands dipped in water. Place some salt inside the side of jar, put the lid on or cover, and shake it around, coating all sides and bottom of jar or crock with a salt layer.

HELPFUL TIPS:

It is important that your miso is packed tightly, free from oxidation and protected by the salt layer. The cloth will also help to keep out impurities and unwanted bacteria.

Label your crock/jar with the date.

Store the jar in a cellar, basement or other cool, dark spot where it will remain undisturbed.

Have patience and ferment for one year. (See "miso years" above.)

Open, scrap off top layer and celebrate with family and friends…your very first batch of homemade miso!! It should smell rich and savory like tamari.

Pack it in clean, glass jars with plastic lids and refrigerate or store in a cool place.

MISO & TEMPEH

Pack the miso into the crock/jar with clean hands, press down firmly. Spread a generous layer of salt over the top. Place the flat object on top and put the weight on top of that. Cover with cloth and secure well with a tight rubber band, string or tape.

You have the option to continue the fermentation process, and like with fine wine, it only gets better with time. If you decide to continue fermentation for another year it is good to test it out and repack it again with salt.

Miso years are calculated by the number of summers it has aged. So, if you have gone through one summer of fermentation, then you have one year old miso. I like to start my miso projects in the spring time, so they are ripe and ready to experience the warmer temps of summer when they tend to be more active.

*You can make this recipe using soy beans as well. Just be sure to use organic soy, since there is less chance of genetically modified contamination.

Contributed by Shira Locarni (superfoods-for-superhealth.com.com)

Shira Locarni's passion and love for fermenting foods, like miso and tempeh, began over a decade ago in pursuit of healthier cooked food alternatives. Shira created the website, Superfoods for Superhealth, "a how-to resource and motivational health guide" incorporating all the many components to diet she has personally found to be extremely beneficial in her own life and those she counsels.

WHAT IS KOJI AND WHERE CAN I FIND IT?

Koji is a Japanese rice on which koji mold spores have been cultivated. This process allows for the fermentation of koji rice, which is the primary ingredient in sake. Although koji spores can be bought, they usually have to be bought from specialty importers. However, fermented koji rice that has already been inoculated with the spores can be found at your local Asian grocery.

WHAT IS TEMPEH & HOW DO YOU INCUBATE IT?

Shira Locarni Says...

Tempeh is a fermented bean cake that is high in enzymes and, because it's been pre-digested by the Rhizopus oligosporus culture, is a good digestible protein source. There is nothing quite like the taste of fresh, homemade tempeh! The best part about making it is that you get to use any bean you want, not just soy bean. Over time, you will discover your favorite legumes and combination's. You can also add cooked grains, like millet and wild rice, as well as a variety of spices and seaweeds. My preferred bean to use is the garbanzo, instead of traditional soy bean. Here is a basic, but delicious, recipe to get you started on your way to "tempeh heaven!"

One of the most important things about making tempeh is that the temperature needs to remain consistent at about 85-90 degrees Fahrenheit (29-32 degrees Celsius), during the 24 hour incubation process. There is some room, however, for slightly lower temps at night we have noticed. The goal is to create an environment of warmth and moisture to encourage fermentation.

Incubation can be achieved in several ways:

1. Dehydrator - we leave our tempeh on top (not inside) of our Excalibur dehydrator on the very lowest temp setting. This ensures heat, but not too much. You don't want to put it IN the dehydrator because this will, of course, dry it out.
2. Oven - place inside an oven for 24 hours on lowest temp with the door cracked open slightly.
3. Cabinet - incubate tempeh in a warm, high cabinet space that is right over your wood stove or other heat source.
4. Greenhouse - if you live in a warm climate, sometimes a greenhouse will even work.

NOTE: You can also pack your tempeh mix into a plastic bag with fork holes, pressing it into a big rectangular shape. This method also allows the tempeh to "sweat" and incubate nicely. We don't promote the use of plastic close to your food, but in a pinch this method works well.

Take pleasure in the delights of this rich and flavorful fermented bean cake. If you have trouble digesting beans, tempeh is a great alternative because it is predigested for you!

Homemade Garbanzo Tempeh Recipe

3 cups garbanzo beans
2 ½ tbsp vinegar
1 ½ tsp tempeh spore starter

Equipment:
Food processor
Glass baking dish/pan
Big bowl
Aluminum foil

(As with making any of the fermented foods, you need to make sure all is clean and your hands are washed to avoid contamination.)

Soak the garbanzo beans overnight. (You can make this recipe using cooked soy beans as well. Just be sure to use organic soy, since there is less chance of genetically modified contamination.)

Cook them the next morning until soft but still firm (slightly under done). Strain liquid and let the beans cool to body temp.

Pulse process lightly in food processor with some whole beans remaining. Place in bowl, add vinegar and mix with spoon. Add tempeh starter and mix thoroughly.

Place into a glass baking dish or pan. Spread evenly and pack it down tight. Place a piece of aluminum foil on top of dish and poke a number of fork holes in foil. Place a cloth over dish and find a warm place to incubate for 24 hours, between 85-90 degrees.

Contributed by Shira Locarni
(superfoods-for-superhealth.com.com)

HELPFUL TIPS:

Make your homemade tempeh recipe in the morning, so that it has the heat of the day to get the spore culture activated. After the culture has established, it will continue to grow at even at slightly lower temperatures.

In 24-30 hours you will have a delicious garbanzo bean tempeh. You can now cut it up into squares because the white culture has firmed up the bean mixture into a solid form. Do not be alarmed at the fuzzy culture growing on the top of it, this is normal and means it has incubated appropriately. When you slice it, you can wrap it individually in wax paper or stack the tempeh with the top side facing down in a container and store in the fridge.

It should smell pleasant with a rich mushroom-like fragrance. Patches of grey or black coloration mean your tempeh has cultured correctly. If it smells off-putting or has green mold or a slimy texture, discard and try again.

BEVERAGES

Fermented drinks are delicious and full of healthy bacteria. In this section, we'll show you how to make fermented drinks from wheat berries, beets, honey, tea, corn, yuca and more!

Rejuvelac

Makes 1 ½ gallons to use as a beverage or a starter for cheese

½ cup soft wheat or rye berries (or a mixture of both)
Purified water

Soak the grains overnight in a ½-gallon jar. The next morning, drain and rinse the grains.

Sprout the grains for 2 days, rinsing and draining twice a day, doing the last rinse with purified water. Fill the jar with purified water and allow to ferment for 36-48 hours, or until the desired tartness is achieved. Pour the Rejuvelac into a container and store it in the refrigerator.

To make a second harvest of Rejuvelac, fill the jar of sprouted grains with water again, ferment for 24 hours, and pour off the Rejuvelac. To make a third harvest of Rejuvelac, fill the jar with water one last time, ferment for 24 hours, and pour off the Rejuvelac. Discard grains.

Contributed by Cherie Soria (rawfoodchef.com)

WHAT IS REJUVELAC?

Rejuvelac is a fermented grain beverage that can also be helpful in culturing nut and seed cheeses. It costs just pennies to make and is one of the most health-promoting drinks on the planet. It's high in enzymes and contains important *lactobacillus bifidus* - both of which are necessary for good digestion and assimilation.

HELPFUL TIPS:

Chlorinated water will kill the precious bacteria you wish to cultivate, and your beverage will smell rotten. Expect the odor and flavor to change from day to day—the first day being the strongest, with your second and third harvests becoming more tart and lemony. Cherie suggests using second- or third-day Rejuvelac for making cheese, since it is milder in flavor.

So that you have fresh Rejuvelac every day, begin sprouting a new batch of grain every three days. (This will require two large jars covered with plastic mesh and secured with rubber bands.) Discard any leftover Rejuvelac, add one herbal fruit tea bag per quart, and steep two hours, or add a squeeze of lemon with a little sweetener and you have Rejuvelac lemonade!

Cherie recommends beginning with small quantities of Rejuvelac so that your body can become accustomed to its cleansing properties. Eight ounces a day, working up to a quart a day, is adequate for most people.

BEVERAGES   101

Beet Kvass with Ginger/Cayenne
(adapted from 'Nourishing Traditions')

Organic beets, peeled and chopped into 2-inch cubes, approximately *(see amount below)*
Natural salt *(not iodized salt and no anti-caking agents in ingredients) (see amount below)*
Ginger, peeled and sliced in 1-inch pieces
Filtered or spring water *(NOT tap water because the chlorine will kill the beneficial flora)*
   (see amount below)
4 liter pickl-it jar
1/8 tsp or less of cayenne *(optional – added after primary fermentation)*

Primary Fermentation:
The key is to use ⅓ beet volume to ⅔ filtered water (not tap water). Place clean peeled chopped beets into glass jar so that it is ⅓ of the volume. Make sure that the beets are not too small. Add a few small 2-inch chunks of peeled ginger.

Make brine. Add about 1 to 1 ½ tbsp of sea salt per quart – you may prefer more and can adjust for the next batch. Dissolve salt completely. *(cont...)*

WHAT IS KVASS?
Beet Kvass is a slightly effervescent lactic-acid fermented beverage tha you can easily make at home from beets, water and natural salt. It provides several organic acids essential for proper liver function, including glucuronic acid. It is an excellent blood tonic, promotes regularity, aids digestion, alkalizes the blood, cleanses the liver, and is a good treatment for kidney stones and other ailments. It is considered a tonic drink, due to the many health benefits from nutrients, enzymes and beneficial organisms in it. Beet kvass has a pleasant, sour flavor, and is often slightly carbonated or effervescent. Beet kvass, like other lactic acid fermented drinks, is best consumed in relatively small amounts.

HELPFUL TIPS:
Beets should be large and detached from greens for at least a week to concentrate the sugars for great kvass. Choose beets that are at least the size of your fist. You can vary the color of the final kvass by choosing different varieties of beets. The orange beets result in a beautiful orange tonic, chioggia or striped pink/white results in a light pink tonic, and the traditional purple beets results in a deep wine colored tonic. The chiogga and the golden beets are milder in flavor or less "beety."

The beets that are taken out after the 2nd fermentation are pickled – you may find them tasty and if so, save them with a light salt brine. Alternatively you can continue to ferment the beets for a few more days – they will become more "pickled". My kids love them but I don't care for them...see what you think.

102   CULTURED: HOW TO MAKE HEALTHY FERMENTED FOODS AT HOME

Fill brine to the shoulder of the jar. Add airlock with filtered water. Keep out of direct light at room temperature.

Keep this in a warm place for 7-9 days. You may see bubbles forming on the top, which means you have some active cultures starting. Taste it after several days; mine usually takes at least 8 days, maybe longer in cooler weather. It should not taste like salty water.

Secondary Fermentation: (To add some fizz and depth)
Strain the beets and/or ginger out and put the juice back into a flip-top glass bottle (I use a 1-liter bottle).

Optional:
Add less than ⅛ teaspoon cayenne or alternative flavor, seal and let ferment for a few more days, even a week. If it tastes good, then go ahead and stick it in the fridge; it tends to develop better taste over time. This is when it will become richer, deeper in flavor and become fizzier. I prefer to drink it cold.

Contributed by Lisa Herndon (lisascounterculture.com)

• • • • • • •

Basic Mead

Makes 3 gallons

2 gallons of water *(spring or filtered)*
¾ gallon of raw honey
6 lemons, juiced
4 organic black tea bags
1 packet of wine yeast

WHAT IS MEAD?

Mead, or honey wine, is an ancient alcoholic beverage made from fermented honey. Research shows that all traditional cultures had some form of ethanol beverage in their diet. Consuming mead with your meals will assist with digestion.

Included is a basic recipe for mead. Once you get the basic understanding of this brew, you can then play around with the ingredients and make quite the medicinal beverage. As the seasons come and go, I like to include a wide variety of wild fruits, herbs, and spices. As with all alcoholic beverages, they are best consumed in moderation.

BEVERAGES

Equipment:
1 3-gallon carboy *(ideally glass)*
3 gallon stockpot
1 stopper and air lock
Siphon
Funnel
Up to 10 empty wine bottles for aging

Bring 2 gallons of water to just under a boil. Once the water is up to temperature, turn off the heat, add in the tea bags, cover the pot and allow to steep for 15 minutes. Allow the tea to come down to 90 degrees before your next step.

In a small bowl, combine 2 oz. of lukewarm water to the yeast packet. Allow to sit and activate.

Once water has reached 90 degrees, remove the teabags and stir in the honey. Stir until is is totally dissolved.

Pour in the lemon juice and stir to combine. Pour in the water and yeast mixture.

Place a funnel on top of the carboy and pour in the honey-water mixture. Remove the funnel and place the water filled air-lock and stopper. Place a piece of tape with the date onto the bottle and store in a warm dark spot in your home.

Within 24 hours, you should begin to see the airlock bubbling. Allow the honey water to ferment for 5-6 weeks. The longer it sits, the drier (less sweet) it will become. At 5 or six weeks use a siphon* to taste your mead. If you are satisfied with the taste, you can begin to enjoy.

At this point you can simply continue to drink, or "rack" it to age your mead. Siphon into 1-gallon jars topped with airlocks and continue to age for an unlimited amount of time. After your desired amount of aging time, you can then siphon into wine bottles and top with a cork. If you do not wish to age your mead, you can siphon directly from the 3-gallon carboy into wine bottles.

*When siphoning your mead, be mindful not to allow any sediment to go into the secondary bottles.

Contributed by Frank Giglio (frankgiglio.com)

What is Kombucha?

Hi, I'm Hannah Crum, the Kombucha Mamma, master brewer, educator and creator of Kombucha Kamp. Kombucha is an all-natural health beverage, made from fermented tea and a starter culture called a SCOBY. It's chockfull of probiotics and other healthy amino acids. Brewing kombucha at home is a process, a dance if you will, with a living being. Yet it is an incredibly easy and rewarding process. I have been known to say: "If you can make a cup of tea, you can make kombucha!" Why choose kombucha over other fermented foods? Well, you don't have to! Incorporate multiple fermented foods into your diet for optimum benefits.

Cultured Tips!

KOMBUCHA 101

What are the Health Benefits of Kombucha?

- Contains probiotics – provides healthy bacteria
- Alkalizes the body – balances internal pH
- Detoxifies the liver – happy liver = happy mood
- Increases metabolism – revs your internal engine
- Improves digestion – keeps your system moving
- Rebuilds connective tissue – helps with arthritis, gout, asthma, rheumatism
- Boosts energy – helps with chronic fatigue
- Is high in antioxidants – destroys free-radicals that cause cancer
- Aids healthy cell regeneration

Why Should Kombucha be the Star of My Fermented Cast?

It's the most versatile. Kombucha can be enjoyed at any time of day; before, during or after meals. Plus, it can be flavored from sour to sweet to savory and more.

It's the easiest to make. Set it and forget it. Literally as easy as making tea.

It's the least expensive. Kombucha can be made for about 10 cents a serving. There are two methods to brew Kombucha, and while many people start with batch brew, most find that continuous brewing is the easiest long term.

What is the Difference between Continuous Brewing vs. Batch Brewing?

In the batch brewing method, you brew a bunch of sweet tea and combine with a little bit of

BEVERAGES

delicious starter liquid - a super sweet 9:1 solution. (90% sweet tea to 10% starter liquid). After 1-2 weeks, the SCOBY and starter liquid work very hard to transform the 90% sweet tea into Kombucha. Continuous Brew makes it much easier.

When you've used about 25% of the CB Kombucha, just refill the brewer with sweet tea. There is no mess and the SCOBY is not contaminated. 75% of your brewer will be mature Kombucha and SCOBY - this time a powerful 3:1 concentration in favor of the Kombucha. It will take only a day or two to transform that small amount of sweet tea into healthful Kombucha. How much you are consuming dictates how often you need to top off your system. It really is the easiest method!

Find Out More About Continuous Brewing by visiting kombuchakamp.com

There is another added benefit to Continuous Brewing - more healthful acids are expressed in the fermentation process, both at the 15-day mark and again at 30 days. In a Batch Brew, the KT would most likely be way too sour to be enjoyable at either of those times. However, with the CB method, because not all of the KT is removed, you receive the benefits while tempering the flavor with younger Kombucha.

Why Should I Continuous Brew Kombucha?

• It's easier. Just pour tea on top. Clean only 1-2 times a year.
• It's faster and you get more. Brewing cycle is reduced to 1-2 days.
• It's healthier. Continuous Brew mixes old with new for delicious Kombucha with more healthful benefits.
• It's better tasting. You can customize flavors, making the tea from sweet to tart.
• It's fun. Tap a glass whenever you want!

You can find Continuous Brewing packages at renegadehealth.com/kombucha.

How Should I Drink Kombucha?

• Drink it straight up; ice mellows the flavor.
• Drink it mixed with juice, soda, or water - add a splash or mix it half and half. This is especially good for batches that taste too tart.
• Drink it mixed with alcohol. It alleviates symptoms associated with hangovers, detoxifies the liver, and just flavors well with spirits.

How Much Kombucha Tea Should I Drink?

Starting with 4 oz. in the morning on an empty stomach is the best way to observe the direct effects that Kombucha has on your system. Follow with water. Drinking water is critical to the cleansing of toxins. Without water, your body will reabsorb them. If drinking the first 4 oz. of kombucha goes well, try another 4 oz. serving before dinner.

106   CULTURED: HOW TO MAKE HEALTHY FERMENTED FOODS AT HOME

Then, listen to your body. If you find you crave it, have some. Should you experience a healing crisis (rash, headache, depression, runs, etc.), cut back the amount you are consuming and drink more water until the reaction subsides (usually a day or two). This is normal. As the toxins release into your bloodstream, they may express in these symptoms.

TIPS: Drinking kombucha 20 minutes prior to your meal will help to curb your appetite. Or drink it after meals to improve digestive function. If you drink "too much" Kombucha, you will just pee or poo it out. Kombucha is best consumed in small, frequent doses rather than in large quantities.

Contributed by Hannah Crum (kombuchakamp.com)

Hannah Crum, known worldwide as The Kombucha Mamma, is the creator of Kombucha Kamp, is a Master Brewer, educator and mentor to 1000s of homebrewers. Learn to brew healthful, delicious kombucha; find out more about Continuous Brewing ("The Ancient Method"); keep up on the kombucha industry news; and, enjoy videos, podcasts and brewing secrets at www.KombuchaKamp.com.

• • • • • • •

Basic Kombucha (continuous brewing)

Makes 2.5 gallons

1 cup organic cane sugar
4-6 bags tea per gallon *(or 4-6 tsp of loose leaf tea)*
Starter cultures, or SCOBYs
1-2 cups starter liquid *(Kombucha - best, or non-raw apple cider vinegar - better, or white non-raw vinegar - good)*
Purified water *(spring, distilled, filtered or boiled)*

Equipment:
Tea kettle or pot to boil the water
Brewing vessel - glass, stainless steel or oak *(with spigot)*
Cloth cover & rubber band - NO CHEESECLOTH; the weave is too loose.

Boil 1 gallon of purified water in a large pot. When the water just starts to a boil, add the tea to the pot. Again, scale the tea depending on the size of your vessel. For a 1 gallon vessel, use 3-5 tsps. Multiply the number you use by the size of your vessel. For a 2 ½ gallon vessel, it would be 6-10 tsps.

Remove from (or just turn off) burner and let steep for 5-10 minutes. After steeping the tea, remove spent leaves and add sugar. 1 cup per gallon = 2 cups for a 2.5 gallon sized vessel. Stir mixture with a spoon until sugar is completely dissolved.

Pour the tea and sugar mixture into the brewer, filling the brewer to about ¾ the way up with the water. Leave a couple of inches of space from the top of the brewer for the culture to grow.

BEVERAGES

Test the water with your hand to make sure that it is below body temperature (lukewarm). Add 2 full-Size kombucha cultures (SCOBYs) and starter liquid. Cover with a 100% cotton cloth, secure with a rubber band.

Allow to ferment for 8-14 days. When you are ready to try it, pour yourself a sip from the spigot Taste once a day until the flavor is just the right mix of sour and sweet for you.

Contributed by Hannah Crum
(kombuchakamp.com)

• • • • • • •

Raw-men with Kombucha Broth

1 butternut squash
3 cups of kombucha
2-3 shiitake mushrooms
1 radish
1 piece of raw coconut
1 piece of raw papaya
Parsley or green onion to taste

(Optional)
Fresh thyme, basil, rosemary, garlic cloves
Cayenne or chili powder

Using a spiralizer, cut a piece of the butternut squash into 'noodles.' If you don't have a spiralizer, cut the butternut squash into thin strips.

Pour Kombucha over the 'noodles.' Add the shiitakes. (For an enhanced flavor, cover and let sit in the fridge for 24 hours. The 'noodles' grow soft and meaty.) Add your garnishes: radish = fish cake, coconut and papaya = boiled egg, parsley or green onion for color and flavor. Spice it up!

Contributed by Hannah Crum
(kombuchakamp.com)

WHERE DO YOU GET A KOMBUCHA CULTURE OR SCOBYS?

SCOBY stands for Symbiotic Culture of Bacteria and Yeast, and it's the mother culture from which kombucha tea is brewed. The traditional way to obtain a SCOBY is through a friend who brews kombucha, but you can also grow your own from a market-bought kombucha brew or by obtaining a culture starter kit.

The best part? With each new batch of kombucha you brew, you create a new SCOBY that can be reused for future batches. You can purchase one from Renegade Health at renegadehealth. com/kombucha.

HELPFUL TIP:

To give the Raw-men with Kombucha Broth a richer "meatier" flavor, you could use rooibos in the primary fermentation stage. Since KT needs camellia sinesis to thrive, I recommend only using a small amount instead of the rooibos along with your tea to impart a smoky flavor.

Kombucha Kocktails

Kombucha's greatest strength is its versatility: healthy beverage, marinade, salad dressing and even cleaning fluid to name a few uses. How about "Drink Mixer" too?! Yes, Kombucha pairs perfectly with liquor, plus it's a natural liver detox. That means when you add Kombucha to the mix, you get a little antidote with your poison.

• • • • • • •

'The Kombucharita" Kombucha Margarita (not virgin)

1 ½ oz Tequila
1 oz Triple sec
1 oz Kombucha
½ oz Lime Juice
5 blueberries *(optional)*

Fill a low ball glass with ice, then dump the ice into a shaker. Combine all ingredients in shaker with ice. Cover and shake vigorously. Pour back into low ball and garnish with lime.

Contributed by Hannah Crum (kombuchakamp.com)

• • • • • • •

Kejiwa Kombucha: SanctiTea Tree Elixir
(Holy Kombucha - As seen on the Travel Channel's 'Bizarre Foods')

The inspiration for this brew comes from the understanding and experience of utilizing mother nature's herbal blessings, delivered through fermented elixir alchemy, to deepen one's relation with the earth, cosmic creator, and one's own soul. This is the intention and meaning behind the name Kejiwa: Falling Into Soul Truth.

THE KOMBUCHA TASTES DELICIOUS, NOW WHAT DO I DO?
Drink from the tap. Pour a fresh glass in the morning or whenever you need a "booch break". Flavor by adding juice. Or...

Decant into bottles. I recommend starting with four, 6-16 oz. bottles at a time. Once you have a fully mature brew, pour the flavoring agents into the bottle, and then fill the bottle up to almost the very top so that little air is left. Screw on the cap tightly to seal in the carbonation. Leave out of the fridge for 2-3 days in a dark place. After a couple of days, taste, and if the flavor is to your liking, move to the fridge to maintain. Monitor and burp the bottles as necessary.

BEVERAGES

1 ½ cups organic cane sugar OR raw local honey
Starter culture plus 1 cup kombucha liquid
1-inch stick palo santo wood
6 tbsp tulsi (holy basil)
3 tbsp yerba santa
3 tbsp (3 teabags) yerba mate
3 tbsp (3 teabags) Roibos red tea
¾ filtered water *(preferably local spring water)*

Equipment:
Stainless steel pot
1-gallon glass or unstained ceramic wide-mouth jar
Strainer
Wooden stirring spoon
Natural fiber 1' x 1' square cloth
Rubber band
pH meter *(optional)*

Coldsteep Yerba Mate for 5 minutes, then strain.

Bring ¾ of a gallon of your local springwater to a boil. Add all herbal tea ingredients and cover the pot. Turn off stove and leave to simmer for 15 minutes. Strain out all solid particles, saving the palo santo wood. Pour the tea into your gallon jar to the bottom of the curve.

Add sugar and stir (For honey, wait until it's lukewarm). Add palo santo stick to the brew, then put cloth cover on, using the rubber band to seal it. Let cool to room temperature (about 12 hours).

Add starter culture and 1 cup kombucha liquid (culture may float to the surface or sink). Ensure the palo santo is below the culture. Cover, seal, and date, placing a prayer and intention. Store in a low-light to dark place (preferably with crystals, sacred geometry, high vibration objects). The ideal temperature range for storing is 70-88 degrees (the warmer the faster the fermentation). Feel free to dance, meditate, laugh, chant, and sing around your kombucha!

(cont...)

WHAT IS PALO SANTO WOOD?
Palo Santo wood has been used by shamans and medicine people for ages as a tea or incense to clear environments, access higher states of consciousness, and develop a deeper connection.

WHAT IS TULSI?
Tulsi is one of the most sacred herbs in India as illustrated by their naming the plant after the Hindu expressions of Divinity (Rama, Tulsi, Krishna Tulsi and Vana Tulsi). You can purchase some at renegadehealth.com/holybasil.

WHAT IS YERBA SANTA?

Himalayan Pink Salt comes

Yerba Santa has been an important medicine for the natives of the Southwest as well as a saving grace for the Spaniards, hence the naming Yerba Santa (Holy Herb). Yerba Santa helps many respiratory issues and in general deepens the breath, bringing health, harmony, and a fuller state of presence.

Check on your kombucha after 10 days (average fermentation between 10-14 days) by testing the pH. Target pH is between 2.9 and 3.2 (The more fermented, the lower the pH). By Taste: If the brew is too sweet, it needs to ferment longer.

To harvest pour out kombucha liquid into a glass container with a lid, remembering to leave at least 1-2 cups liquid with your culture and the newly formed culture. To build up carbonation and strengthen the brew, leave capped container in same fermentation place for 1-3 days, checking to make sure not too much pressure has built up in the container. Note: Your brew will get stronger!

Put in the fridge to slow the fermentation – until your preferred taste! Now you have 2 cultures to start 2 new batches – Congratulations!

Contributed by Illup Gravengaard (kejiwa.com)

Illup Gravengaard's first meeting with Kombucha was a bit of a baptism, being blessed by half the bottle of a store-bought beverage. Soon he was honored with the presents of a home-brew and was blown away by the difference; the smoothness, the vitality, the love and dedication that came through full fortitude!

CAN YOU GIVE ME SOME TIPS ABOUT STORING MY KOMBUCHA CULTURE?

Illup Gravengaard Says...

You can store multiple cultures in one container with a fabric covering (called a kombucha hotel) at room temperature or for an extended period in the fridge. Just make sure they don't dry out!

You can handle the cultures with clean hands and gently peal apart the mother and new culture to separate.

To avoid mold from forming, don't ferment in the same area as potted plants! Although mold is a very rare occurrence, it will be obvious; you'll see white or green fuzzy circles.

Always avoid storing kombucha in metal containers, and never use metal spoons!

Yeast is a natural bi-product of the fermentation, and it looks like brown squigglies. Even though they're harmless, staining them out is best. Don't move the container too much during fermentation, as doing so will slow the process by unsettling the new growth.

You can absolutely compost your culture...If your culture is no longer vibrant – your compost will love it! You can also turn the culture into a fun new art project, like drumheads, frisbees, or fashion accessories!

Chicha de Maiz (Corn Chicha)

2 ½ cups fresh, organic corn *(off the cob)*
½ cup strawberries
½ cup coconut sugar
10 cups water
1 packet Body Ecology culture starter *(or your favorite culture starter)*

In a large pot, combine the corn and water. Place over high heat and bring to boil, stirring now and then with a wooden spoon and scraping the bottom of the pot to prevent sticking and burning. When the mixture comes to a full boil, lower the heat and gently simmer, covered, for 2 hours, stirring now and then. Remove from heat and allow to cool.

Once cool, strain off the corn and set the corn water aside.

Put 1 cup corn, ½ cup of strawberries, and 1 cup of corn water in blender. Blend well, then strain through a nut milk bag. Add this juice to the remaining corn water, along with the sugar and culture starter. Poor into airtight glass containers and place in a dark place at room temperature. Let ferment for 2-5 days, depending on how strong you like it. Garnish with a lemon slice.

Contributed by Annmarie Gianni (RenegadeHealth.com and AnnmarieGianni.com)

SEE HOW TO MAKE CHICHA DE MAIZ:
RENEGADEHEALTH.COM/CULTURED/CORN

WHAT IS CHICHA?

Chicha is a fermented corn drink that has been a flavorful part of Peruvian cuisine for centuries. The ancient Inca would drink it as a ceremonial beer during many of their rituals, and today it can be found at many roadside stalls in Peru. It is said to lower blood pressure and reduce inflammation in the body.

BEVERAGES   *113*

Chicha de Yuca (or Yuca Chicha)

2 yuca (cassava) – medium size
1 sweet potato or yam
1 ripe plantain or banana
16-18 cups water
Your favorite culture starter *(optional)*

Bring your water to a boil. As you wait for the water, peel the yuca and sweet potatoes and cut into chunks. Place the yuca and sweet potatoes in the boiling water and let them cook for about 20-30 minutes or until soft. You can tell when they are done when you can put a fork in them. Remove from the heat and let cool down until luke warm.

Scoop out the root veggies and place them in a blender with the plantain and a little bit of the boiled water. Blend on high speed. Then mix the yuca paste with the same liquid that it was cooked in. Next, slowly mix in your culture starter.

Pour into glass airtight containers and place in a dark place at room temperature. Let ferment for 2 to 5 days, depending on how strong you like it. We like it strong!

Contributed by Annmarie Gianni (RenegadeHealth.com and AnnmarieGianni.com)

SEE HOW TO MAKE CHICHA DE YUCA:
RENEGADEHEALTH.COM/CULTURED/YUCA

HOW DO I PEEL A YUCA?

Dip the yuca root for 2 minutes in boiling water. This is an optional step, but helps to soften the peel. Place the yuca on a cutting board. With a towel on top of it, press firmly down on the yuca. Do this a few times. This again will help soften the peel. Make a long vertical cut along the root with a sharp knife and lift one side, peeling away any skin that comes off easily. Remove the rest of the skin from the root with a sharp potato peeler. Your sharp paring knife also can do the job, although this may require more work. Your goal is so you only see the white of the vegetable!

Chicha de Quinoa

1 oz cinnamon bark
¼ tsp ground clove
10-12 cups water
¾ cups quinoa flour
¼ cup brown rice flour
½ cups coconut sugar
Your favorite culture starter *(optional)*

Boil water in a saucepan with the cloves and cinnamon. Add in quinoa and rice flour slowly, stirring constantly to avoid lumps and to incorporate in the cinnamon water. Simmer for 20 minutes. Let cool and strain, once cool add sugar.

Pour into glass airtight containers and place in a dark place at room temperature. Let ferment for 2 to 5 days, depending on how strong you like it.

Contributed by Annmarie Gianni (RenegadeHealth.com and AnnmarieGianni.com)

SEE HOW TO MAKE CHICHA DE QUINOA:
RENEGADEHEALTH.COM/CULTURED/QUINOA

Authentic Pineapple Chicha

This is a recipe I learned from an old woman in the rainforest of Honduras. Our guests at Casa Verde LOVE CHICHA because it's very refreshing, full of enzymes and oh so…GOOD! Plus, the ingredients are normally something you would have put in the compost; I LOVE being able to use them for NOURISHMENT instead!

Rinds of 1 whole pineapple
Core of same pineapple
Sweetener of choice *(optional)*
1 tsp finely sliced ginger *(optional)*

Put rinds and core of the whole pineapple into a 2-liter glass pitcher. Cover well. Put in a cool, dark place (like a cabinet). Let sit quietly for 4-6 days (the darker the place and the longer it sits, the stronger it will be).

BEVERAGES

After 4-6 days, take a look…the top of the liquid should be scummy and a smell a little funky. No worries; this means it's READY! Strain the liquid through a sieve. Discard the rind and core.

If you prefer your Chicha sweet, add sweetener of choice and stir well. Personally, I like it straight and tart! As an alternative, add finely sliced ginger for a spicy boost!

Contributed by Wendy Green
(wendygreenyoga.com)

Wendy Green took her first yoga class in Boston in 1973 and found it was an immediate "fit", About the same time, she began teaching yoga at the now famous Hippocrates Health Institute in Boston, where she became the head of their Raw Food kitchen for 2 years under the direction of Dr Ann Wigmore and Victorus Kulvinskus. She cashed out of the states in 2005, found a gorgeous property in the rainforest of Hondruas and offers RAW YOGA CLEANSING RETREATS in a pristine, spectacular environment.

HELPFUL TIP:
Warning DO NOT PUT ANY CHICHA IN THE BLENDER… once fermented the chicha is slightly carbonated and will EXPLODE!

GLUTEN-FREE BREADS

In this section, you'll discover how to make two traditional breads (carbohydrateS) of India and Ethiopia. We're pleased to bring these exciting recipes to you so that you can experiment and try these gluten-free options at home!

Injera

1 cup teff flour
1 ½ cup pure water
¼ tsp salt
½ tsp aluminum-free baking soda *(or baking powder if you want it more sour; the baking soda neutralizes less of the acids)*
1 tbsp coconut oil

Mix the flour and water in a bowl. Let it sit with a towel over the top in a warm place in the house for 1-4 days, depending on how fermented you want it. When you are ready to cook it, add salt and baking soda. You may want to add a little water to create a thin consistency.

Heat an iron skillet and add the coconut oil. Pour a very thin layer of batter on the hot skillet. Cover with a lid and let it cook until there are holes all over the injera. You won't flip it, so keep it on the skillet until the top is dry. This requires the batter to be spread to a consistent thinness and the pan to a perfect temperature.

Now it is ready to eat! You can keep it warm in the oven.

Contributed by Summer Bock (summerbock.com)

WHAT IS INJERA?

Injera is a fermented yeast-risen bread made with a small grain called teff. This spongy, tasty bread is eaten traditionally in Ethiopia and Eritrea. Teff is gluten-free, but many restaurants that serve injera make their bread with added wheat flour. You can serve injera with traditional Ethiopian food, but also can experiment with raw, steamed or sauteed vegetable dishes.

GLUTEN-FREE BREADS
119

Idlis

2 cups white basmati rice
1 cups red lentils

Cover lentils and rice in water and soak for 1-3 days, depending on air temperature. Strain the rice and lentils. Grind them into a batter in a blender or food processor, adding only a small amount of water (as needed) to blend it into a thick and creamy paste. Ferment for another 1-3 days. It will rise and bubble. Once the batter has fermented, add a pinch of salt to it.

Slightly oil each idli steamer mold and spoon the batter into the molds of the steamer. Steam, covered, for exactly 20 minutes. Idlis should be firm. Remove the idlis from the molds.

Serve with anything - from chutneys to stews, in bento boxes or with soup, or create desserts with them!

Contributed by Summer Bock (summerbock.com)

WHAT ARE IDLIS?

Idlis are south Indian rice and lentil cakes that are cooked by steaming. They're traditionally served at breakfast or as a snack with chutney.

In order to make idlis, you'll need a specialized piece of equipment that looks kind of like an egg poacher. It is called an idli steamer, and you can order it from specialty Indian food stores.

DESSERTS

What's better than a delicious, healthy dessert? A delicious, fermented, healthy dessert!
This section will highlight many different kinds of cultured snacks - from savory to sweet.

Sweet Probiotic Fruit Chutney

This is a great topping for cashew cream, oatmeal, or for a great raw cobbler.

1-quart wide-mouthed mason jar
3 cups of organic fruit* *(peaches, nectarine, plums, mango, or apples)*
¾ - 1 cup kefir water *(see page 72)*
Grated rind of 2 lemons
Juice of 2 lemons
3 tsp spices *(I usually use fresh, coarsely ground cinnamon & nutmeg)*
2 tsp himalayan sea salt
1-2 tbsp honey or maple syrup *(optional; the fruit is usually sweet enough on it's own)*
½ cup nuts and raisins *(optional)*

Mix lemon juice, rind, sweetener, spices, salt and kefir. Combine with chopped fruit. Stir in optional nuts and raisins.

Place in mason jar. Press down lightly, adding more kefir to cover the fruit (You can also add some fresh juice from the fruit). Mixture should come to 1 inch below the top of the jar. Cover tightly, and keep at room temperature for 2 days, then transfer to fridge. Use within 2 months, or freeze for up to 12 months.

* Expect any food that has been fermented/cultured to triple the vitamin and mineral content. So, if you cannot use organic produce, the fermenting process detoxifies the produce so that it is harmless.

Contributed by Naomi Hendrix (rawfresno.com)

• • • • • • •

Fermented Nut & Seed Cheesecake

This cheesecake is so good that you won't believe it's so good for you. Fermenting nuts and seeds is easier than it sounds, and you can get some delicious results that help your gut heal! The crust is optional, but makes a nice presentation if you want a real cheesecake look.

Cheesecake Ingredients:
2 cups macadamia nuts, soaked overnight
2 cups Brazil nuts, soaked overnight
1 cup Real Food. Real Life. Lime Mint flavor Pro-Belly-Otic *(probiotic liquid)*, or your
   favorite probiotic powder.
2 tbsp coconut oil
4 tbsp ghee
2 tbsp vanilla extract

DESSERTS 123

1 cup natural sweetener *(Lokanto, erythritol and xylitol made from birch are great options that do not feed candida yeast.)*
2 tsp sea salt

Crust Ingredients:
1 ½ cups almonds *(soaked for 8-12 hours and drained)*
1 cup ground flax seeds *(Soaked 8-12 hours. The mixture will be thick and sticky from the water absorbing in. This will help hold the crust together. Drain off excess water.)*
4 tbsp raw almond butter
4 tbsp coconut oil
1 cup natural sweetener *(Lokanto, organic erythritol and xylitol made from birch are great options that do not feed candida yeast.)*
2 tbsp vanilla extract

Preparation:
Soak all nuts and seeds for 12-24 hours. Either put each nut and seed in its own separate glass bowl to soak, or combine the macadamia and Brazil nuts in one bowl and the flax seeds and walnuts in another bowl. (To soak, cover nuts with water and leave out in a covered glass container. This removes the anti-nutrients in nuts and seeds that makes them difficult to digest).

After soaking, drain water from the nuts and seeds and rinse. (Note: you won't have to drain the flax seeds because the water will have absorbed and made a gel/paste like consistency. This is good because it helps everything stick together without having to use raisins or dates, which are often too sweet for people with candida yeast).

Cheesecake Filling Preparation Directions:
Put the macadamia and Brazil nuts into a food processor (with the 'S blade') or high speed blender (if you have a Vitamix, Blendtec or high speed blender, you can often get a more "whipped" consistency. This can be nice but is not necessary). Blend it up smooth.

Add in the Pro-Belly-Otic and blend. Some fermented nut recipes use Rejuvelac, which can be problematic for people with candida yeast issues. Instead, I like to use the Lime Mint Pro-Belly-Otic because it is fermented from organic, healthy grains and seeds that can help colonize your gut with good bacteria, which helps improve digestion. Real Food. Real Life. products are high quality, raw, organic, vegan, kosher probiotic whole food products that use some of the hardiest probiotics on the market. Because they are whole food, the probiotics also have a better chance at making it past your stomach acid and into your intestines, where they can do their work. Adding these high quality probiotics is necessary to ferment your nuts and seeds. If you do not have any Real Food. Real Life. products on hand, you can use the powder from some probiotic capsules (about 1 tbsp, or about 16 capsules). I prefer to have a very medicinal end product that is full of hardy probiotics, so I like whole food probiotic sources.

Let this mixture sit in a covered, air tight glass container for 24 hours. You can leave it on your countertop (do not refrigerate). This will allow the nuts to ferment. After 24 hours, pour the mixture back into your blender or food processor or blender. Add the natural sweetener, coconut oil, ghee, sea salt and vanilla and blend up. Taste and see if you need to add anything else (like natural sweetener, a pinch of sea salt, more ghee to give it a dairy-like flavor, or more vanilla). Make sure you like the taste before continuing with the recipe. Everyone's tastes are a bit different. Set aside in the refrigerator until you are ready to add to the crust.

Crust Preparation Directions:
Put almond butter and flax seeds into your food processor with the 'S blade' or blender and blend up smooth. Add remaining ingredients and blend up.

Press mixture about 1 inch thick into a pie dish or baking pan. Add cheesecake filling on top and chill in the refrigerator for at least 2 hours before serving. Enjoy!

Contributed by Heather Fougnier (nowradianthealth.com)

· · · · · · ·

Cultured Cacao-Wows

2 ½ cup raw, organic cacao powder
½ cup cacao butter
½-1 cup coconut sugar
1 tbsp Vitamineral Green powder
1 packet Body Ecology kefir starter
1 packet Body Ecology culture starter

WHAT IS CACAO?
IF you've had chocolate before – which would be just about anyone reading this! – then you're familiar with cacao, the raw fruit of the cacao tree from which both chocolate and cocoa are made. It's found in South America and the Caribbean.

WHAT IS VITAMINERAL GREEN?
It is an extremely potent and comprehensive green powder suppliment that contains an array of nature's most nutritive and cleansing superfoods, grown and processed to maximize their benefits. It contains a full spectrum of naturally occurring, absorbable and non-toxic vitamins, minerals, all the essential amino acids (protein), antioxidants, chlorophyll, soluble and insoluble fibers, tens of thousands of phytonutrients, and a plethora of other synergistically bound, organic nutrients. You can purchase some at renegadehealth.com/vg.

DESSERTS   *125*

(Add-ins)
Sea salt, cacao nibs, and mesquite; cherries, cayenne and sea salt; maca, mesquite and
lucuma; cinnamon, maca, mesquite and lucuma; spirulina and mint; Goji berries, bee pollen
and anything else you like with your chocolate!

Equipment:
Glass jar or bowl with lid
Candy molds of choice
Blender

Melt cacao butter at 80 degrees in food dehydrator, then stir in cacao powder. Blend mixture
with coconut sugar in blender. then pour into glass jar. Add green powder and culture starters.

Let ferment for 36 hours, then add your choice of add-ins. Pour into molds, refrigerate and enjoy!

Contributed by Gina LaVerde (blissedlife.com)

• • • • • • •

Fresh Fruit Pro-sicles™

Makes 6-8

1 peach, cut into ½-inch slices *(½ cup)*
2 kiwis, peeled and sliced into ¼-inch rounds *(¾ cup)*
¾ cup strawberries, finely chopped
½ cup fresh blueberries
½ cup fresh raspberries
1 ½ cups coconut water
¼ cup (two, 1 oz. servings) Grapefruit flavor Pro-Belly-Otic™ *(Or, you can use coconut kefir.*
   See page 73.)

Combine fruit in a mixing bowl, then divide the mixture into 6-8 molds. Combine coconut
water with Pro-Belly-Otic™, and pour enough into each mold to just cover fruit. (If there's not
enough liquid, add more coconut water.) Insert popsicle sticks and freeze until solid (about six
hours). To release, run popsicle molds under cool water for a few seconds, then gently pull out.

Contributed by Tamara Yapp (realfoodreallife.tv)

Tamara Yapp is an entertaining health advocate and change catalyst, and she is the founder and
CEO of Real Food. Real Life, a company that is dedicated to bringing the best products and
information to people everywhere so they can lead healthier lives physically, emotionally, and
socially. Through the video episodes and information she shares on RealFood.RealLife.TV, as
well as the products she creates, Tamara's goal is to help people take realistic steps to leading
healthier lives and to shorten the learning curve.

CULTURED: HOW TO MAKE HEALTHY FERMENTED FOODS AT HOME

HELPFUL TIP:

Note that these quantities are only guidelines. Some people like to make the popsicles sweeter by adding more honey, or more chocolaty by adding more cocoa or cacao. I even know a few people who add a little extra salt to get that sweet/salty taste.

Orange-Mojita Pro-sicles™

2 oranges, peeled and finely chopped
1 cup lime juice *(from approximately 6-8 limes)*
¼ cup filtered water
¼ cup *(two, 1 oz. servings)* Lime-Mint flavor
    Pro-Belly-Otic™ *(Or, you can use coconut kefir. See page 73.)*
6-10 drops liquid stevia to taste *(I like SweetLeaf™ orange-flavored stevia but any will do.)*
4 sprigs mint

or...

Avocado-Chocolate Pro-sicles™

4 medium avocados, peeled and pitted
1 cup coconut milk
½ cup water *(may need more)*
¼- ⅓ cup organic honey
5-7 tbsp unsweetened cocoa or cacao powder
2 tsp organic vanilla extract
Pinch of sea salt
¼ cup *(two, 1-oz servings)* Great Grains flavor
    Pro-Belly-Otic™ *(Or, you can use coconut kefir. See page 73.)*

Makes 6-8

Combine all ingredients except Pro-Belly-Otic™ and blend until smooth. (For the Avocado-Chocoloate 'sicles, add in the cocoa or cacao and salt last, blending until creamy.) Then, add Pro-Belly-Otic™ and blend lightly. (You may need to add more water to achieve the right consistency.) Pour into 6-8 molds. Insert sticks and freeze until solid - about six hours. To release, run popsicle molds under cool water for a few seconds, then gently pull out.

Contributed by Tamara Yapp
(realfoodreallife.tv)

PART III
CONTRIBUTORS & INDEXES

CONTRIBUTORS

MEET THE AWESOME CULTURED TEAM

Summer Bock

Summer Bock is a fermentationist and owner of OlyKraut, a small artisan company, which has been rooted in Olympia since 2008. They hand make each batch of fermented vegetables using organic ingredients sourced from as close to home as possible. Their seasonal approach to processing captures the peak of taste and abundance at harvest time. They use time-honored preservation techniques that enhance nutritional value, celebrate the power of raw tradition, and provide living food all year round. Filled with probiotics like Lactobacilli, their refreshing raw kraut strengthens immune function, supports digestion, and revitalizes the body after using antibiotics.

As a health coach and herbalist Summer works with nutrition enthusiasts to thrive in their own health so they can coach their clients better and create practices that help change the world! "Nutrition Nerds" are people who are already on the healing path, have nutrition books like, Healing with Whole Foods on their nightstand and still struggle with health concerns. Summer helps them to keep their health in tip-top shape so they can spend their precious energy on the important things in life, like family, business, friends, pleasure and their passions.

After years of heavy drug use, Summer came out of a fog with a congested liver and a new lease on life. Dealing with Candida, IBS, chemical sensitivities, environmental allergies, depression, eczema, rashes, food allergies and more--- she detoxed her body and focused on rebuilding her own intestinal ecosystem. This allowed her to heal from all these issues except gluten and dairy intolerance. Now she helps people all over the world accomplish the same results.

Summer is an educator in her community and at the Institute for Integrative Nutrition in NYC. She has certifications and degrees from the New Mexico College of Natural Healing, the Evergreen State College, the Institute for Integrative Nutrition, and Columbia University.

SummerBock.com | OlyKraut.com

OUR AWESOME CONTRIBUTORS: MEET THE CULTURED TEAM

Hannah Crum

Hannah Crum, known worldwide as The Kombucha Mamma, is the creator of Kombucha Kamp, is a Master Brewer, and educator and mentor to 1000s of homebrewers. Her writings and workshops have been featured on the Veria Network as well as in Bev Net, Beverage Spectrum Magazine, Whole Life Times Magazine, Los Angeles Times Best Bets, Elephant Journal, Vital Juice and many more. Learn to brew healthful, delicious Kombucha, find out more about continuous brewing ("The Ancient Method"), keep up on kombucha industry news and enjoy videos, podcasts & brewing secrets at **KombuchaKamp.com** or e-mail her at kombuchakamp@gmail.com.

. . . .

Julie Erwin

As a holistic health counselor and founder of Streamlined Nutrition in Los Angeles, Julie thrives on transforming private and group clients from accidents-waiting-to-happen into vibrant people who have: Learned to eat defensively; learned to listen to what their gut wants, not what their head thinks it wants; lost weight and kept it off; unclogged their metabolisms, intestines, arteries and cells; shifted their sugar blues; arrested their over-eating; curbed their cravings; elevated their energy; navigated dietary theories and learned what works for them; and, stopped spending their retirement on prescription drugs.

Increased vegetable consumption, in particular cultured vegetables, form the foundation of her healthy food and lifestyle programs. Julie has been especially inspired by the work of Donna Gates (*The Body Ecology Diet*) and that of Sally Fallon (Founder of The Weston A. Price Foundation). Julie received her Holistic Health Certification at the Institute for Integrative Nutrition in NYC. Find out more about Julie **streamlinednutrition.com**.

Heather Fougnier

Heather Fougnier, a former executive turned professional health coach and writer, is certified in transforming people's lives through nutrition and energy healing techniques. After 15 years in a fast-paced corporate career, Heather healed long-standing, chronic digestive pain and disordered eating by shifting her diet and mindset. It is her mission to empower people to live happier lives by creating balance in their bodies and successfully (and profitably) doing what they love. You can find her at **nowradianthealth.com**.

Donna Gates

Donna Gates' mission is to change the way the world eats. Over the past 25 years, Donna has become one of the most loved and respected authorities in the field of digestive health, diet, and nutrition, enjoying a worldwide reputation as an expert in anti-aging, weight loss, autism, autoimmune diseases, candida, and adrenal fatigue.

Donna is a nutritional consultant, author, lecturer, home economist and founder of Body Ecology™, Inc., a leading nutrition company. She is the author of Body Ecology Diet: Recovering Your Health and Rebuilding Your Immunity, a revolutionary system of healing that she created in response to the major deficiencies she saw in medicine and the commonplace approach to treating symptoms while ignoring root causes. It is the first of its kind. Filling the void, the diet — sugar-free, gluten-free, and probiotic rich — was adopted by doctors and health practitioners alike, who recommend it to their patients and clients. Donna has certified hundreds of "Body Ecologists" who passionately spread her teachings throughout the United States, Canada, England, Australia and New Zealand. *The Body Ecology Diet: Recovering Your*

Health and Rebuilding Your Immunity has sold nearly a quarter of a million copies and a newly revised edition is now available through Hay House.

As a key figure in the autism movement, Donna works with top doctors in the field who view her diet as instrumental in changing the theory behind and treatment of the disorder. She founded Body Ecology Diet Recovering Our Kids (BEDROK), an active online community of over 2,000 parents, many of who have seen their children in full recovery. Visit www.bedrokcommunity.org.

Donna's free newsletter, available at www.BodyEcology.com, is one of the most respected natural-health publications in the world. Her eagerly anticipated book, *The Baby Boomer Diet*, (Hay House, October, 2011), is expected to revolutionize the way we think about aging. Please visit **bodyecology.com** for more information.

Annmarie Gianni

Annmarie Gianni is an internationally known author, health advocate, and founder of Annmarie Gianni Skin Care. Just a few years ago, Annmarie started to take a hard look at the products she was putting on her skin. In just a few short days of research, what she found shocked her. Skin care products were severely under-regulated and most contained ingredients that weren't safe at almost any amount. Even products that claimed they were organic or natural had hidden preservatives and other nasty additives. She was frustrated and motivated to find a better option because she realized so many people were using these supposedly "natural" products.

What she found was not encouraging. Many of the truly natural products weren't up to her standards of quality or effectiveness. It wasn't long until she realized that if she wanted to have a truly clean and natural skin care line, she would have to do it herself. So she did and Annmarie Gianni Skin Care was founded to provide a clean, natural skin care experience using natural, organic and wildcrafted ingredients. Annmarie now spends her time educating audiences around the United States about how to preserve your beauty and

longevity from the inside out as well as what to look for when you're searching for a skin care line that will keep your skin glowing and vibrant. She can be seen as a regular co-host and chef on the popular online health show "The Renegade Health Show" at RenegadeHealth.com. Annmarie has also trained as a massage therapist, athletic trainer and has run a successful personal training business in Fairfield County, Connecticut. When she's not being a business woman, training others, or hosting her weekly internet show, Annmarie enjoys traveling, being outside and preparing healthy meals. She loves to hike and run in the woods, and spend time with her cat Jonny 5.
RenegadeHealth.com and **AnnmarieGianni.com**

Frank Giglio

Frank Giglio is a classically trained chef from the New England Culinary Institute in Montpelier, VT, a graduate of The Institute for Integrative Nutrition in NYC and worked under the guidance of Dr. Gabriel Cousens at the Tree Of Life Rejuvenation Center in Patagonia, AZ. Since the age of 15, Frank has fully immersed himself into the culinary world. Young and intrigued, Frank went on to apprentice under some of the countries top chefs where he was able to find a deep understanding for the creative process of working with food, as well a learning the fine art of tastes and flavors. With a strong passion for using food as medicine Frank works greatly to produce sustainable cuisine, which to him, means seeking the highest quality foods grown locally and in alignment with the environment. The base of Frank's culinary offerings lie in classic technique and traditional foods preparation. Frank's merging of herbalism, superfood and raw food nutrition with fresh, seasonal and local foods create a cuisine, that is wholesome, pure and full of vitality! For more information, please check out Frank's websites at **FrankGiglio.com** and **FranksFinestLLC.com**.

Jackie Graff

Jackie Graff has been teaching raw food preparation and food science for more than a decade. An RN with 40 years' experience in various areas of patient care and education, Ms. Graff is considered one of the country's top raw food chefs and nutrition consultants. She continues to teach raw food lifestyle classes throughout the country, is an instructor for Hallelujah Acres® Culinary Academy, and at the Hippocrates Health Institute in West Palm Beach FL. She has been frequently quoted in print and broadcast news outlets, including the Atlanta-Journal Constitution, /Atlanta Womanmagazine, Atlanta Jewish Life magazine, Fox 5 Good Day Atlanta, CNN Headline News, and North Georgia Today. Jackie is the author of 23 theme raw food recipe books, and has produced two instructional raw food DVDs. Jackie also contributed articles to several national and local magazines. As an RN, Ms. Graff has held key hospital management positions and was a clinical instructor to nurses. She also served as an associate professor at Life University, teaching raw food instruction to returning alumni. She has an understanding of nutrition, anatomy and physiology of the human body and possesses a firsthand knowledge of the negative consequences of the Standard American Diet (SAD) on a person's long-term health. She earned her B.S. degree in Nursing from the University of South Carolina.

Jackie & Gideon Graff teach a three week certification course in Raw Food Nutrition Science, Health Education, and Raw Culinary Arts Chef Certification. To learn more about becoming certified, visit rawfoodcert.eventbrite.com and homechef.eventbrite.com. Please visit their website **rawfoodrevival.com** for more information about Jackie's recipe books, DVDs and prepared raw food, cookies, drinks, and products.

Illup Gravengaard

Illup Gravengaard's first meeting with Kombucha was a bit of a baptism, being blessed by half the bottle of a store-bought beverage. Soon he was honored with the presents of a home-brew and was blown away by the difference; the smoothness, the vitality, the love and dedication that came through full fortitude! Kombucha was the gateway into finally fully being able to listen to the body wisdom and what was truly being called. Since, Illup has researched and experimented with kombucha and other live foods intensely, along with helping to build — from the ground up — one of the most amazing live organic vegan cafés on the planet, ChocolaTree Organic Oasis. In addition, he has communed deeply with the land of the Southwest; shared his own version of kombucha elixirs on the Travel Channel's 'Bizarre Foods' with Andrew Zimmern; held several dozen kombucha live food wild herbalism classes and workshops; conducted numerous studies utilizing sound healing, chanting, singing, sacred geometry, pyramid technology, and crystal energetics in conjuction with live food production; and, created a company called Kejiwa, which means 'blissfully falling into Your Soul Truth', corralling all the wisdom he has been graced with along the journey. **kejiwa.com**

Wendy Green

Wendy Green took her first yoga class in Boston in 1973 and found it was an immediate "fit", About the same time, she began teaching yoga at the now famous Hippocrates Health Institute in Boston, where she became the head of their Raw Food kitchen for 2 years under the direction of Dr Ann Wigmore and Victorus Kulvinskus. She cashed out of the states in 2005, found a gorgeous property in the rainforest of Hondruas and offers RAW YOGA CLEANSING RETREATS in a pristine, spectacular environment. **wendygreenyoga.com**

OUR AWESOME CONTRIBUTORS: MEET THE CULTURED TEAM

Heather Haxo Phillips

Heather Haxo Phillips is the Principal and Founder of Raw Bay Area. She is an accomplished and passionate raw vegan food chef and Bay Area native. She is the primary raw food instructor for the Bay Area's leading raw restaurant Café Gratitude, as well as several Whole Foods markets in the area. Through Raw Bay Area, Heather offers raw food coaching, classes and special events to inspire and educate people about the power of raw food. Heather is a certified raw food chef/instructor and graduate of the Living Light Culinary Arts Institute. Her holistic approach to food and well-being makes Heather a very popular speaker for participants at all skill levels. Students say Heather's classes are informative, extremely well-presented, easy to follow and fun! You can check out what Café Gratitude says about Heather's classes here: www.cafegratitude.com/our-blog/tags/Heather-Haxo-Phillips. Heather is also a certified Iyengar Yoga instructor, teaching in the East Bay. Before launching Raw Bay Area four years ago, Heather spent 10+ years in the non-profit sector as an executive director, fundraiser and event planner. She is a graduate of Harvard College. **rawbayarea.com**

Naomi Hendrix

Naomi Hendrix grew up on a farm, eating fresh fruit and vegetables daily. At 16 she moved into town and her diet changed. But because of her healthy foundation in life, she sought a healthier lifestyle beginning with vegetarianism, progressing to juicing and green smoothies. Naomi delved into raw food in 2007. She hit a crossroad at this time, when Naomi's son Ian died from a seizure (though she knew in her heart food was what really killed him). She continued eating raw half of the time until she was diagnosed with Dysbiosis in 2009. She understood that all processed foods needed to be eliminated from her diet. She sought out education, learning how to prepare food in a different way. She studied with ImmuneNutrition in Portland, OR and became a Certified Healing Foods Specialist in the Fall of 2010. As a Living Food educator, co-founder and resident chef at Revive Café in Fresno, Naomi continues her journey of learning and teaching how to transition one's lifestyle from a SAD (Standard American Diet) to a Real Food Lifestyle. **rawfresno.com**

Lisa Herndon

Lisa Herndon is quite passionate about "real food" and loves being able to share her recipes and techniques for creating nourishing and traditional foods. She is especially interested and skilled in fermentation and can go on for hours on all the crazy and fun things you can do with ferments while supporting your health and wellness. Much of her inspiration comes from the amazing text, *Nourishing Traditions: The Cookbook that Challenges Politically Correct Nutrition and the Diet Dictocrats* by Sally Fallon and *Wild Fermentation: The Flavor, Nutrition, and Craft of Live-Culture Foods* by Sandor Ellix Katz. Lisa's Counter Culture offers focused hands-on workshops with limited participants to insure proper attention and care for each participant. Each class covers the creation process from start to finish - so even if some of these items take weeks to culture - you will still get a sense of the whole process. The workshops are specially scheduled so that each stage is experienced, giving you a chance to become more familiar and comfortable with the overall process when you start fermenting or cooking at home. **lisascounterculture.com**

Cecilia Kinzie

Cecilia Kinzie discovered raw foods in 2001 and was able to heal from Chronic Fatigue Syndrome and Asthma by adopting a plant based high raw food diet. Her message is that true healing and transformation occurs from the inside out. She believes that the foods we eat and the thoughts and emotions we think and feel can have a huge impact on our well being. Cecilia now teaches people about the healing power of eating whole and organic foods through her website and blog, **rawglow.com** and **rawglow.com/blog**. She is also a meditation teacher and intuitive healer who helps sensitive and intuitive people tap into their inner guidance and soul power to live strong, balanced, and purposeful lives. She can be reached for intuitive healing sessions and guided meditations at www.circleforselfhealing.com. Cecilia currently lives in sunny California with her husband and two beloved Chihuahuas.

Gina LaVerde

Gina LaVerde loves fermented food. Especially chocolate-style fermented food. Her new book *Are You Eating Your Bugs?* reveals how these ultra-healing goodies helped her family recover from autism, candida and seizure disorder. She's a Reiki Master Teacher, Body Ecology Coach, and unschooling mama who runs an autism healing program, and helps clients from all over the world find their Bliss. You can catch her at BlissedLife.com, where she and her family share their journey. They're touring the US by RV right now, and you better believe they're toting plenty of healing treats.

Shira Locarni

Shira Locarni has been involved in healthy living and the healing arts for most of her adult life. Her passion and love for fermenting foods, like miso and tempeh, began over a decade ago in pursuit of healthier cooked food alternatives. Numerous health challenges early in life led her to study and incorporate the principles of The Body Ecology Diet program by Donna Gates. She began the weekly practice of making her own raw sauerkraut and cultured vegetables, which she continues to this day. Shira broadened her involvement in the alternative health field as a Certified Massage Therapist, specializing in Advanced Shiatsu and Acupressure, maintaining her own practice for 14 years. In doing so, she was exposed to a broad array of healing modalities, which led her to pursue apprenticeships in herbal studies at Sage Mountain Herbal Center and Dry Creek Herb Farm. Shira also became a Certified Herbalist and Wholistic Lifestyle counselor through the Evergreen School of Integrative Herbology. This 2-year intensive program "integrated" Chinese, Ayurvedic and Western herbs and dietary approaches. Shira's continued study and emphasis on Chinese tonic herbs sparked an interest in Asian culture and the traditional food ferments such as kim-chi, miso and tempeh, prompting her to seek out ways she could make these foods at home. Shira created the website, **superfoods-for-superhealth.com**, "a how-to resource and motivational health guide" incorporating all the many components to diet she has personally found to be extremely beneficial in her own life and those she counsels.

• •

Brian James Lucas (Chef BeLive)

Brian James Lucas is one of the pioneers of the 90s gourmet raw food movement. From 1998 to '99, Brian was Executive Chef and co-owner of Organica: the Living Cuisine, located in San Francisco, CA. Organica was unique in that it was one of the first gourmet raw living restaurants in the world that was completely raw, vegan and organic (wild or biodynamic). The restaurant was definitely ahead of it's time, as you will find characteristic of Brian.

Chef BeLive placed as one of the top chefs in the world in the Best of Raw contest for 2008 and 2009, as well as received the #1 Favorite Gourmet Raw Chef Award for 2010. He considers himself a "transitional" gourmet raw chef, specializing in creating raw living cuisine that tastes superb, thereby helping make people's first experience with raw living foods equal to many of their cooked favorites. He has encouraged a multitude of people to discover a healthier diet through flavorful raw living plant based cuisine, including a number of athletes, actors and politicians. Chef BeLive has a unique style that is definitely his own, which has gained him praise amongst his peers and an increasingly large fan base.

Chef BeLive was featured in Carol Alt's new raw food book, *The Raw 50*, where you can find the recipe for his "Mom's Stuffed Bells." He is also the author of the ebook, *Orgasm of the Taste Buds*, which has 30 delicious and simple recipes. Both the recipe, as well as his ebook, can be found on his website **ChefBeLive.com**.

Jill Nussinow

Jill Nussinow, aka The Veggie Queen™, and alternative Registered Dietitian, shares food and nutrition insights from a vegetarian and vegan perspective. She advocates a high raw diet, demonstrating how to ferment and sprout foods on a regular basis. Jill has been teaching people about the joy of eating vegetables since 1985. She showcases her work on her website **theveggiequeen.com** and at cooking classes, workshops and lectures throughout the United States and beyond. She enjoys spreading culture through the art of fermenting foods.

Rene Oswald

René Oswald is an RN and an Advanced Practitioner of Health. Working as a nurse for many years, she suddenly found herself with a rare, incurable auto-immune disease called Mastocytosis. After searching for many years, she found the answer to health to be in the food she ate. René completed course work at the Optimum Health Institute, where she witnessed how raw foods could restore health. René and her husband Allan developed the "Transitioning to Living Cuisine" program, which is a gradual progression to healthy eating, written in 7 levels. All of her recipes are raw, vegan, sugar-free, wheat-free, gluten-free, and dairy-rree. She has also written the eBooks *Juice Feasting for Life*, *Living Cuisine for Happy Holidays* and *Wholesome Cooked Creations* and her entire TLC program is also available in eBook form. Find full descriptions at reneoswald.com/ebooks.html. René has been teaching Living Foods Preparation Classes and Seminars since 2002. She believes that everyone should have the opportunity to experience maximum health in their lifetime and she loves helping others achieve their health goals. **rawfoodrene.com**

Jessica Prentice

Jessica Prentice is a professional chef, author, local foods activist, and social entrepreneur. Her first book, *Full Moon Feast: Food and the Hunger for Connection*, was released by Chelsea Green Publishing in 2006. Jessica is a co-creator of the Local Foods Wheel, and coined the word "locavore." Jessica is also a co-founder of Three Stone Hearth (**threestonehearth.com**), a community supported kitchen in Berkeley that uses local, sustainable ingredients to prepare nutrient-dense, traditional foods on a community scale. She lives, works, and writes in the San Francisco Bay Area.

Dr. Cate Shanahan, M.D.

Dr. Cate Shanahan, M.D. studied genetics at Cornell University before Medical School. While in Hawaii she identified four culinary traditions shared by her longest-lived patients, described in *Deep Nutrition: Why Your Genes Need Traditional Food*. In 2010, she developed T.R.I.M. (Treatment to Reverse Inflammatory Metabolism), a unique weight-loss program. Visit **DrCate.com** for popular recipes.

Nomi Shannon

Nomi Shannon is an award winning author and world renowned coach. Her best selling book, *The Raw Gourmet*, has sold over 165,000 copies. Her second book, *Raw Food Celebrations* (with S.Duruz), is flying off the shelves at bookstores worldwide.

In 2008 Nomi received three Best of Raw Awards for Best Raw Educator, Favorite Raw Chef and Favorite Raw Book. In 2009s and 2010s Best of Raw Awards, Nomi placed in the top 5 in many categories including: Best Educator, Chef, Blog, Online Store and her personal favorite, Funniest Raw Woman.

She's not only a certified Hippocrates Health Educator, but she actually ran The Hippocrates Health Institute's Certification Course back in the early 1990s.

Raw since 1987, Nomi has been featured in Alive magazine, Get Fresh, San Diego North County Times, Galveston News, as well as numerous radio shows and other media.

Nomi is known for teaching people proven steps to keeping — or regaining — vibrant health. Her website www.rawgourmet.com offers breakthrough information, product reviews, delicious recipes, an ezine and an online course, all free of charge. She also offers online coaching courses, her books, raw kitchen equipment, DVDs, phone consultations and live classes.

Since there's conflicting information about what's the "best" raw food diet, many raw fooders wonder what to eat. Nomi shows people a simple path to thriving on raw food and leaving the confusion behind. Just as important, she empowers people to whip up delicious meals quickly and easily, turning newbies into thriving home chefs practically overnight.

RawGourmet.com
YourRawFoodDiet.com
WhatDoRawFoodersEat.com

Cherie Soria

Cherie Soria is founder and director of Living Light Culinary Institute and author of 3 books including, *Raw Food Revolution Diet*. Known as the mother of gourmet raw cuisine, Cherie has been the inspiration of a generation of raw food chefs and authors. She began teaching vegetarian cuisine nearly 40 years ago and has been teaching raw vegan culinary arts for 20 years to students from over 50 countries. Cherie and her husband, Dan Ladermann, also own three other award-winning, eco-friendly businesses on the north coast of California, including the Living Light Café, Living Light Marketplace, and the Living Light Inn.

Visit Cherie's website for information about certification courses in raw culinary arts and the science of raw food nutrition for individuals, chefs, and instructors. **RawFoodChef.com**

Novalee Truesdell

Novalee Truesdell received a double BA in German and Psychology from Lipscomb University in Nashville, TN. She later interned at Kushi Institute and studied at LLCAI in Fort Bragg, CA. Nova has also completed Doug Grahams Raw Nutritional Science course. She first got into juicing and raw foods when she worked in the Natural Living department, stocking books on cleansing, teaching people how to follow through with those programs, as well as doing demos of them. She now works with Discountjuicers.com, an on-line company that sells all your raw food appliances, and films videos on how to use them to make fabulous raw food recipes.

Besides raw food, Nova's passion is animal rescue and dog training. She is a Certified Animal Trainer with certification from ABC (Animal Behavioral

College). Nowadays you can find Nova teaching, working as a raw food personal chef, as well as experimenting with and teaching raw food for dogs classes. Nova teaches raw food prep and gardening at **youtube.com/enovalee**.

Wendy Valley

Wendy Valley resides in West Central Florida, where she operates an in-home retreat center for those desiring instruction in adopting a plant-based diet. She also works with John P. Monhollon, M.D. at the Florida Integrative Medical Center. Her greatest passion, however, rests in the Perfect Pickler Company, which she co-owns with company founder, Bill Hettig. With her canning jar fermentor, The Perfect Pickler, you make your own rich probiotic pickles for pennies in just 4 days! **perfectpickler.com**

Tamara Yapp

Tamara Yapp is an entertaining health advocate and change catalyst, and she is the founder and CEO of Real Food. Real Life, a company that is dedicated to bringing the best products and information to people everywhere so they can lead healthier lives physically, emotionally, and socially. A shining example of someone who has taken life's challenges and made, well...not lemonade, but something better: her probiotic liquids and powders and an edutainment TV show that helps people everywhere, Tamara says: "It is not what happens to you in life that creates who you are. It is how you handle it that creates your life. I spent years looking for something to help my son, and found that I could create something that could help almost everyone."

In the late '90s, soon after her young son CJ was diagnosed with autism, colitis and crohn's disease, Tamara spent years devoting her life to caring for him.

A woman on a mission who does not take "no" for an answer, Tamara interviewed the top doctors and leading experts in both traditional and alternative medicine and health to find ways to make CJ and the rest of her family healthier.

Through learning about many different diets and nutritional philosophies, Tamara discovered the wonder of fermented, pre-digested foods and liquids that are filled with probiotics. She integrated them into CJ's and the rest of her family's diet and continuously saw amazing results. Today, CJ is a strong and healthy, growing teenager and communicates well with his family again. Tamara's health and that of her entire family has vastly improved since she began incorporating fermented probiotic foods and the other life-enhancing practices and foods into their lives.

Through the video episodes and information she shares on RealFood.RealLife.TV, as well as the products she creates, Tamara's goal is to help people take realistic steps to leading healthier lives and to shorten the learning curve.

Tamara, a 50-year-old mother of seven and Los Angeles native, resides in Southern California with her music industry executive husband Jeff Yapp, their two youngest children, horses and dogs. When she isn't researching and testing products for her company, she enjoys spending time with her family and friends. **realfoodreallife.tv**

RECIPE INDEXES

SUBJECT, RECIPE, CONTRIBUTOR

Index: by Subject

A

alcohol 7, 23, 105
  beer v, 7, 9, 71, 112
  margarita 108
  mead 5, 102, 162, 167
  wine iii, 5, 7, 9, 78, 95, 101, 102, 103
allspice 55
almond butter 123, 124
almonds 77, 79, 80, 81, 84, 85, 87, 123, 150
amino acids iii, 13, 16, 17, 18, 19, 36, 70, 85, 88, 104, 124, 150
ancient Earth Minerals See Body Ecology
anise 34, 37
antipasto 66, 161, 169
apples 5, 8, 37, 39, 40, 46, 47, 48, 106, 122, 150
apple cider vinegar 5, 46, 106
avocado 41, 44, 45, 52, 150

B

bacteria iii, iv, vii, 4, 5, 8, 10, 12, 13, 14, 16, 18, 20, 22, 23, 25-27, 30, 33, 35, 37, 39, 40,
    41, 46, 50, 51, 52, 54, 56, 58, 59, 64, 70, 75, 90, 91, 94, 99, 100, 104, 107, 23
banana 66, 113
banana peppers 66
basil 43, 44, 85, 87, 88, 107, 109, 150, 154
basmati rice 119
beer See Alcohol
beets 34, 46, 48, 50, 53, 99, 101, 102, 150
black pepper 55, 156
VitaMix 39
blueberries 108, 125, 150
Bock, Summer 49, 62, 118, 119, 132, 166
Ancient Earth Minerals See also Body Ecology
Body Ecology vi, 38, 70, 133, 134, 135, 141 See also Gates, Donna
  Ancient Earth Minerals 39
  Body Ecology culture starter 32, 33, 34, 39, 46, 50, 58, 81, 112, 124
  Body Ecology kefir starter 71, 72, 124
  EcoBLOOM 39
bok choy 32, 60, 151
bread, gluten-free
  Idlis 119, 162, 166
  Injera 118, 162, 166

INDEX BY SUBJECT

brine 9, 26, 27, 32, 35, 39, 40, 41, 43, 49, 53, 55, 58, 62, 63, 64, 66, 67, 94, 101, 102

C

cabbage 8, 9, 10, 22, 23, 30, 37, 40, 46, 49, 52, 54, 60
  green cabbage 32, 34, 39, 47, 48, 50, 51, 55, 58
  napa cabbage 52, 58, 59, 62
  purple cabbage 40, 42, 51, 52
  red cabbage 34, 43, 47, 48, 50, 53
cacao
  cacao butter 124, 125, 151
  cacao powder 124, 125, 126
caraway 34, 37, 46, 48, 53
cardamom 37, 42, 151
carrots 9, 32, 40, 42, 44, 48, 49, 50, 52, 58, 60, 62, 151, 160, 168
cashews 77, 80, 84, 87, 88, 89, 151
cauliflower 52, 151
cayenne 42, 52, 58, 59, 60, 101, 102, 125, 151, 156
celery 34, 40, 42, 46, 49, 50, 64, 91, 151
cheese iii, 10, 89, 91 See Nut Cheese
  Cheese Balls 91
  curd cheese 89, 91
cheesecloth 65, 66
Chef BeLive See Lucas, Brian James
chicha 112, 113, 114, 115, 162, 166, 167
chicory root 39
chili pepper 59, 64
chipotle powder 55
cilantro 40, 44, 45, 56, 151, 154
cinnamon 51, 79, 80, 81, 114, 122, 125, 151
coconut
  coconut kefir See Kefir
  coconut meat 77, 78, 81, 89, 107, 152
  coconut milk 74, 126
  coconut oil 80, 118, 122, 123, 124, 152
  coconut, opening 78
  coconut sugar See Sweeteners
  coconut syrup See Sweeteners
  coconut water 8, 71, 73, 78, 81, 125, 152
corn 7, 9, 10, 26, 41, 46, 91, 99, 112, 157
Crum, Hannah 104, 106, 107, 108, 133, 166
cucumber 42, 45, 47, 56, 61, 63, 64, 65, 66, 71, 91, 152
culture starter 27, 32, 34, 39, 40, 46, 50, 58, 70, 72, 81, 107, 112, 113, 114, 124 See
      also Body Ecology Culture Starter
cumin 32, 58

curds 8, 76, 90, 91
curry 37, 42

D

daikon 40, 49, 58, 59, 60, 62, 89
dairy kefir See Kefir
dandelion 44, 152, 154
dates 32, 34, 35, 57, 58, 79, 88, 123, 152, 153
dessert
  Cacao-Wows 124, 163, 168
  Fermented Nut & Seed Cheesecake 122, 123, 163, 166
  Sweet Probiotic Fruit Chutney 71, 122, 163, 167
  Fresh Fruit Pro-sicles 125, 126
dill 34, 43, 46, 50, 56, 64, 65, 86, 152, 154
dill seed 34, 64
dried onions See Onions
dulse 32, 33, 34, 35, 42, 50, 58, 152, 160, 168

E

E3 Live 74
EcoBLOOM See Body Ecology
eggs 15, 17
  hard boiled 56
Erwin, Julie 41, 133, 166

F

fennel 39, 40, 51
fermentation ii-vii, 4, 5, 7-10, 12-20, 19, 22-26, 30, 31, 33, 38, 39-41, 43, 46, 48-52, 54-
    56, 60, 61, 62, 67, 69-72, 74, 75, 76, 78, 80, 81, 84, 85, 89, 90, 92, 95-97, 100-102,
    104-105, 107-112, 115, 118-119, 121-123, 132, 140-141, 148
flax seeds 123, 124
Fougnier, Heather 30, 42, 43, 44, 80, 124, 134, 166

G

garbanzo beans 94, 97
garlic 9, 32, 34, 35, 40, 42, 44-46, 48-52, 55, 58-62, 64-66, 85, 86, 107, 153, 160, 168
garlic powder 42
Gates, Donna vi, 38, 39, 133, 134, 141, 166
ghee 122, 124
Gianni, Annmarie 81, 112, 113, 114, 135, 166

INDEX BY SUBJECT   *153*

Giglio, Frank 66, 103, 136, 166
ginger 9, 32, 37, 40, 43, 44, 49, 51, 52, 58, 59, 60, 61, 62, 71, 101, 102, 114, 115, 153
glycemic index 36, 41
Graff, Jackie 50, 60, 64, 137, 167
Gravengaard, Illup 110, 111, 138, 167
green cabbage See Cabbage
green onions See Onions
Green, Wendy 115, 138, 167

𝓗

Harsch crock 32, 33, 35, 58
Haxo Phillips, Heather 72, 73, 78, 79, 87, 139, 167
hemp seed 42, 52, 154
Hendrix, Naomi 45, 122, 139, 167
herbs
  basil 43, 44, 85, 87, 88, 107, 109, 150, 154
  chicory root 39
  cilantro 40, 44, 45, 56, 151, 154
  dandelion 44, 152, 154
  dill 34, 43, 46, 50, 56, 64, 65, 86, 152, 154
  fennel 39, 40, 51
  parsley 42, 49, 56, 86, 87, 107, 154, 156
  rosemary 87, 88, 107
  tannic leaves 65, 66
  thyme 44, 50, 88, 107, 154, 159
Herndon, Lisa 75, 76, 140, 167
Himalayan crystal salt 36, 37, 59, 85 See also salt
holy basil See tulsi
Holy Herb See Yerba Santa
honey See Sweeteners

𝓘

idlis See Bread, Gluten-free
injera See Bread, Gluten-free
Institute for Integrative Nutrition 41, 66, 132, 133, 136
Italian seasoning 66

##

jalapeño 44, 45, 154, 157

K

kale 39, 40, 155
kefir 69–72
  coconut kefir 24, 43, 52, 73, 74, 79, 125, 126, 152, 161, 167
  dairy kefir 70, 75, 161, 167
  Strawberry Nectarine Kefir Sorbet 74
  water kefir 44, 45, 71, 72, 87, 122, 161, 167
  kefir starter 70, 71, 72, 73, 124 See also Body Ecology kefir starter
kelp 42, 43
kimchee 58, 161, 168 See also Kimchi, Kim Chee, Chee
kim chee 59, 60, 161, 167, 169 See also Kimchi, Kimchee, Chee
kimchi g, 9, 57, 61, 161, 168 See also Kimchee, Kim Chee, Chee
Kinzie, Cecilia 52, 74, 140, 167
koji 92, 94, 95
kombucha ii, iii, 5, 23, 27, 76, 104-111, 133, 138, 162, 166, 167
kraut See Sauerkraut
kvass 101, 162, 169

L

LaVerde, Gina 46, 74, 125, 141, 167
lemon juice 32, 34, 35, 46, 58, 65, 67, 87, 89, 103, 122
lemons 46, 71, 102, 122
lentils 119
Living Light Culinary Arts Institute 36, 72, 139
Locarni, Shira 92, 95, 96, 97, 141, 168
lokanto See Sweeteners
Lucas, Brian James 81, 88, 89, 142, 168

M

mandoline 36, 89
mango 45, 122, 155
margarita See Alcohol
mead 5, 102, 162, 167
milk iii, 4, 8, 23, 74, 75, 76, 77, 78, 81, 87, 89, 90, 112, 126, 150, 154, 155, 156, 157, 158
mint 39, 74, 125, 126, 155
miso g, iii, 8, 9, 23, 85, 87, 92, 93, 94, 95, 141, 142, 155, 162, 168
mushroom 97, 155
mustard seeds 65

INDEX BY SUBJECT

N

napa cabbage See Cabbage
nori 50, 156
Nussinow, Jill 53, 61, 143, 168
nut cheese 46, 84, 85, 162, 169
  Almond Cheese 85
  Cashew Cheese 84
  Cultured Cheese 88
  Herbed Almond 'Chèvre' 87
  Herbed Cheese Spread 86
nutmeg 42, 85, 87, 122, 156
nutritional yeast 85, 156

O

Okroshka 56, 161, 168
olive oil 38, 41, 67, 85, 88
olives 66
onions 9, 45, 48, 49, 53, 62, 66
  dried onions 88
  green onions 52, 56, 61, 65, 86, 88, 107
  red onions 36, 43, 44, 59, 65, 86
  spring onions 60
  sweet onions 39
Oswald, René 33, 34, 59, 143, 168

P

palo santo wood 109
papaya 107, 156
paprika 34, 55, 86
parsley 42, 49, 56, 86, 87, 107, 154, 156
parsnip 48
peppers 9, 52, 55, 66, 156, 157
pickles 47, 63, 64, 65, 66, 67, 70, 147, 161, 167
  Pickle Relish 65, 161, 169
pickling spice 64, 65
pineapple 74, 114, 157
pomegranate 40, 157
Prentice, Jessica 54, 55, 144, 168
Pro-Belly-Otic 43, 79, 80, 122, 123
probiotic powder 65, 72, 80, 84, 122
Pro-sicles See Dessert
purple cabbage See Cabbage

156   CULTURED: HOW TO MAKE HEALTHY FERMENTED FOODS AT HOME

R

radicchio 40
radish 40, 49, 56, 59, 89, 107
rapadura See Sweeteners
raspberries 79, 125, 157
red cabbage See Cabbage
red onions See Onions
red peppers 52
Rejuvelac 80, 87, 100, 123, 162, 169
rosemary 87, 88, 107

S

salt 17, 26, 32, 34-39, 41-45, 49, 51-55, 58-62, 64-67, 79, 80, 85, 87-89, 94, 95, 101,
    118, 119, 122-126, 151, 154, 157, 158
sauerkraut 5, 6, 8, 9, 24, 25, 32, 33, 34, 35, 47-55, 58, 59, 62, 142, 160, 161, 167-169
scallions 55, 157
SCOBY 70, 104, 105, 107
sea vegetables See also seaweed; See also wakame; See also dulse; See also nori; See
    also Silky Sea Palm
seaweed 33, 47, 48
shallots 40
Shanahan, Dr. Cate 56, 91, 144, 168
Shannon, Nomi 47, 48, 145, 168
Silky Sea Palm 51
snap beans 66
Soria, Cherie 36, 37, 60, 65, 80, 84, 86, 100, 146, 169
sour cream g, 89, 162, 168
spices
  allspice 55
  anise 34, 37
  black pepper 55, 156
  caraway 34, 37, 46, 48, 53
  cardamom 37, 42, 151
  cayenne 42, 52, 58, 59, 60, 101, 102, 125, 151, 156
  cayenne powder 42
  chili pepper 59, 64
  chipotle powder 55
  cinnamon 51, 79, 80, 81, 114, 122, 125, 151
  cumin 32, 58
  curry 37, 42
  garlic powder 42
  Italian seasoning 66

INDEX BY SUBJECT

157

mustard seeds 65
nutmeg 42, 85, 87, 122, 156
paprika 34, 55, 86
pickling spice 65
turmeric 49, 62, 159
spring onions See Onions
squash 44, 107, 158
stevia See Sweeteners
strawberries 74, 79, 112, 125, 158
sucanat See Sweeteners
sugar See Sweeteners
sweeteners 36, 41, 79, 80, 81, 100, 115, 122, 123, 124
  coconut sugar 22, 65, 81, 112, 114, 124, 125
  coconut syrup 36, 81
  honey 5, 7, 22, 78, 81, 99, 102, 103, 109, 122, 126, 154, 158
  lokanto 36, 40, 41
  rapadura 40, 41
  stevia 36, 41, 79, 80, 81, 100, 115, 122, 123, 124, 126
  sucanat 40, 41
  sugar vi, 17, 22, 23, 26, 38, 39, 41, 50, 52, 61, 65, 70-72, 81, 106, 109, 112, 114, 124,
        125, 133, 134, 144, 150
  xylitol 36, 79, 123
sweet onions See Onions
sweet potatoes 43, 113

𝒯

tannic leaves 65, 66
teff flour 118
tempeh iii, 9, 56, 93, 95, 96, 97, 141, 142, 162, 168
thyme 44, 50, 88, 107, 154, 159
thyroid 33, 42
Tomatillos 67
Tomatoes 45, 88
  dried tomatoes 66
  green tomatoes 66
Truesdell, Novalee 51, 52, 102, 146, 169
tulsi 109
turmeric 49, 62, 159

𝒱

Valley, Wendy 67, 147, 169
vanilla 74, 78, 79, 81, 122, 123, 126

vegan cheese See Nut Cheese
Vitamineral Green 124

W

wakame 47, 50
water 74, 75
  distilled water 64
  filtered water 32, 35, 43, 55, 58, 64, 66, 67, 76, 88, 101, 102, 109, 126
  purified water 80, 84, 85, 100, 106
  spring water 44, 45, 65, 101, 109
Water Kefir See Kefir
whey 56, 65, 66, 71, 89, 90, 91
wine See Alcohol, Mead

X

xylitol See Sweeteners

Y

Yapp, Tamara 125, 126, 147, 169
yerba santa 110
yogurt 77, 78, 81, 89
  Almond Yogurt 79
  BeLive's Almond Coconut Yogurt 81
  Cashew Yogurt 80
  Vanilla Coconut Yogurt 78
yuca 99, 113 See also Chicha

Z

zucchini 44, 45, 50, 89, 160

Index: by Recipe

Vegetables & Sauerkrauts

Applekraut 37
"Beet It" Fermented Beet Salad 46
Bok Choy Carrot Crunch 32
Cultured Vegetable-Sea Vegetable Energy Soup 42
Detox Energy Soup 44
Dilly Dulse Kraut 6
Doubly Red Kraut 53
Garlic Caraway Kraut 34
Jackie's Juniper Vege-Kraut 50
Korean Vegetable Pickle 52
Lacto Fermented Salsa 45
Mixed Kraut 48
Okroshka 56
Orange Cultured Vegetables 40
Peter Piper's Kraut 55
Pickled Pink Cultured Vegetables 43
Pickled Red Onions 36
Purple Cultured Vegetables 40
Red or Green Sauerkraut 47
Savory Sauerkraut Breakfast Bowl 52
Scarlet Cultured Vegetables 34
Simple & Fresh Culutred Vegetables 39
Spicy Zucchini Spears 44
Super Simple Sauerkraut 51
Tangy Coleslaw 49
Veggie Kraut 48

Kimchi

Basic Kim Chee 59
Daikon Kimchee Kraut 58
Sprout Kim Chee 60
Watermelon Rind Kimchi 61
Spicy Turmeric Chee 62

Pickles

Crunchy Pickles 66

Fermented Dill Pickles 64
Pickled Antipasto 66
Sweet Pickle Relish 65

Kefir

Classic Vegan Water Kefir 72
Dairy Kefir 75
Green-ya Coladas 74
Vegan Coconut Kefir 73
Strawberry Nectarine Kefir Sorbet 74

Yogurt

Almond Yogurt 79
BeLive's Almond Coconut Yogurt 81
Cashew Yogurt 80
Strawberry Jam 79
Vanilla Coconut Yogurt 78
Yogurt 81

Cheese & Sour Cream

Basic Nut Cheese 84
BeLive's Cashew Sour Cream 89
Cultured Cheese 88
Curd-Cheese & Fermented Whey 89
Herbed Almond 'Chevre' 87
Herbed Cheese Spread 86
Italian Pesto Almond Torte 85
Mini Raw Ravioli 88
Smokin' Cheese Balls 91

Miso & Tempeh

Homemade Garbanzo Miso Recipe 94
Homemade Garbanzo Tempeh Recipe 97

Beverages

Authentic Pineapple Chicha 114
Basic Kombucha 106
Basic Mead Recipe 102

INDEX BY RECIPE

Beet Kvass with Ginger/Cayenne 101
Chicha de Maiz 112
Chicha de Quinoa 114
Chicha de Yuca 113
Kejiwa Kombucha: SanctiTea Tree Elixir 108
Kombucharita 108
Raw-men with Kombucha Broth 107
Rejuvelac 100

Gluten-free Breads

Injera 118
Idlis 119

Desserts

Avocado-Chocolate Pro-sicles™ 126
Cultured Cacao-Wows 124
Fermented Nut & Seed Cheesecake 122
Fresh Fruit Pro-sicles™ 125
Orange-Mojita Pro-sicles™ 126
Sweet Probiotic Fruit Chutney 122

Index: by Contributor

Summer Bock

Idlis 119
Injera 118
Spicy Turmeric Chee 62
Tangy Coleslaw 49

Hannah Crum

Basic Kombucha 106
Kombucharita 108
Raw-men with Kombucha Broth 107

Julie Erwin

Orange Cultured Vegetables 40
Purple Cultured Vegetables 40

Heather Fougnier

Almond Yogurt 79
Cultured Vegetable-Sea Vegetable Energy Soup 42
Detox Energy Soup 44
Fermented Nut & Seed Cheesecake 122
Pickled Pink Cultured Vegetables 43

Donna Gates

Simple & Fresh Cultured Veggies 39

Annmarie Gianni

Chicha de Maiz 112
Chicha de Quinoa 114
Chicha de Yuca 113
Yogurt 81

Frank Giglio

Basic Mead 102
Crunchy Pickles 65

INDEX BY CONTRIBUTOR

Jackie Graff

Fermented Dill Pickles 64
Jackie's Juniper Vege-Kraut 50
Sprout Kim Chee 60

Illup Gravengaard

Kejiwa Kombucha: SanctiTea Tree Elixir 108

Wendy Green

Authentic Pineapple Chicha 114

Heather Haxo Phillips

Classic Vegan Water Kefir 72
Herbed Almond 'Chevre' 87
Strawberry Jam 79
Vanilla Coconut Yogurt 78
Vegan Coconut Kefir 73

Naomi Hendrix

Sweet Probiotic Fruit Chutney 122
Spicy Zucchini Spears 45
Lacto Fermented Salsa 45

Lisa Herndon

Dairy Kefir 75
Beet Kvass with Ginger/Cayenne 101

Cecilia Kinzie

Savory Sauerkraut Breakfast Bowl 52
Strawberry Nectarine Kefir Sorbet 74

Gina LaVerde

Cultured Cacao-Wows 124
"Beet It" Fermented Beet Salad 46
Green-ya Coladas 74

Shira Locarni

Homemade Garbanzo Miso Recipe 94
Homemade Garbanzo Tempeh Recipe 97

Brian James Lucas (Chef BeLive)

BeLive's Almond Coconut Yogurt 81
BeLive's Cashew Sour Cream 89
Cultured Cheese 88
Mini Raw Ravioli 88

Jill Nussinow

Doubly Red Kraut 53
Watermelon Rind Kimchi 61

René Oswald

Bok Choy Carrot Crunch 32
Daikon Kimchee Kraut 58
Dilly Dulse Kraut 34
Garlic Caraway Kraut 34
Scarlet Cultured Vegetables 34

Jessica Prentice

Peter Piper's Kraut 55

Dr. Cate Shanahan

Curd Cheese & Fermented Whey 89
Smokin' Cheese Balls 91
Okroshka 56

Nomi Shannon

Red or Green Sauerkraut 47
Mixed Kraut 48
Veggie Kraut 48

Cherie Soria

INDEX BY CONTRIBUTOR

Applekraut 37
Basic Kim Chee 59
Basic Nut Cheese 84
Cashew Yogurt 80
Herbed Cheese Spread 86
Italian Pesto Almond Torte 85
Pickled Red Onions 36
Rejuvelac 100
Sweet Pickle Relish 65

Novalee Truesdell

Korean Vegetable Pickle 52
Super Simple Sauerkraut 51

Wendy Valley

Pickled Antipasto 66

Tamara Yapp

Avocado-Chocolate Pro-sicles™ 126
Fresh Fruit Pro-sicles™ 125
Orange-Mojita Pro-sicles™ 126

A Simple Approach to Health, Eating, and Saving the Plan...

KEVIN GIANNI'S

High Raw

Kevin Gianni, internationally known health advocate, author, and producer of the hit internet TV blog, The Renegade Health Show, debunks a common myth about health—He teaches that it DOESN'T have to be hard!

Enter a New, Simple Paradigm of Health

With five easy principles, *High Raw* clears the confusion about nutrition science and gently encourages you to effortlessly create a lifestyle of sustainable health.
Are you ready to enjoy your health journey every step of the way? Are you ready to feel your best now AND in the future? Are you ready to feel more connected in mind and body to your community, and to the planet? If the answer is 'yes,' then get ready, get set, go! The time is now.

Start Your High Raw Journey Today!

DOWNLOAD YOUR FREE COPY TODAY:
WWW.GOHIGHRAW.COM